MW00807326

What's Your Catholic IQ?

22 Faith Quizzes for All Ages

Page McKean Zyromski

Pflaum Publishing Group
Dayton, OH

Cover and Interior Design by Kathryn Cole
Edited by Karen Cannizzo

The Scripture quotations contained herein are from the *New Revised Standard Version Bible*: Catholic Edition, ©1993 and 1989 by the Division of Christian Education of the National Council of the Churches of Christ in the U.S.A. Used by permission. All rights reserved.

©2006 Pflaum Publishing Group. All rights reserved. Photocopying of the material herein is permitted by the publisher for noncommercial use. The permission line must appear on each reproduced page. No other use of this text is granted without written permission from the publisher.

Second Printing: 2006

Pflaum Publishing Group
2621 Dryden Rd., Suite 300
Dayton, OH 45439
800-543-4383
www.pflaum.com

ISBN 978-1-933178-36-3

Contents

Rookie   Almost-Expert   Scholar

Catechesis Through Quizzes = Fun Faith Formation

Testing ourselves is a national pastime! We also like to watch others test themselves. Today's most popular TV shows test physical prowess and endurance or ingenuity and business skills.

Quiz shows and game shows test for overall knowledge. We're all proud when we guess correctly before the contestant answers. We groan "I should have known that!" when we're wrong. But whatever the outcome, we win because either we feel pretty smart or we learn something new.

That's also the goal of this book. Catholics of all ages can test themselves on how well they know their Church. If they know the answer to a question, they feel pretty good. If they don't know the answer, they learn it. Everybody wins!

Use these quizzes as discussion starters rather than written exercises. Lead the group through a quiz. Discuss each question, and give everyone a chance to answer. If the group gets stumped, then give the answer and explain it. That helps participants learn—and have fun while doing it.

Why Use This Book?

Kids learn while having fun.
Kids have fun testing themselves. They can even use the quizzes to create their own game shows.

The Bible becomes more user-friendly.
Scripture stories and quotes support the quizzes and help participants become more familiar with the Bible. For deeper, personal study, Scripture citations point the way.

Intergenerational activities enrich all.
One generation helps another work through the quizzes. All ages reach a deeper understanding of one another and of their faith.

Catechist/parent meetings turn lively.
Break the ice at your next catechist or parent meeting with a faith quiz. Participants connect as they work together to answer the questions.

Sacrament prep turns into family fun time.
Parents and children help one another complete a sacrament quiz. There's no pressure on one person when families come together to share the answers. Everyone has something to contribute.

Family night becomes "fun with faith."
Encourage parents not to "peek" at the answer sheets. If they quiz themselves along with their children, everyone will learn more.

Seven Faith Categories
- Advent-Christmas
- Bible
- Catholic Identity
- Commandments–Beatitudes
- Lent-Easter
- Sacraments
- Saints

Three Levels in Each Category
Rookie, Almost-Expert, and Scholar
- Choose a level that fits your group.
- Icons mark each quiz. Only you know the level you chose.
- Watch Rookies quickly become Scholars—and take on the Bonus Round!

1. The word *Christmas* comes from
(a) *Christ's Mass* (b) *Emmanuel* (c) *Yule*
(d) *Hosanna*

2. Mary wrapped Jesus in swaddling clothes and laid him in a manger because
(a) mangers were fancier in those days
(b) sleeping on hay was thought to be good for a person's health (c) there was no room in the inn (d) none of these

3. The group of mysteries of the rosary that includes the Nativity is
(a) the Joyful Mysteries (b) the Sorrowful Mysteries (c) the Glorious Mysteries
(d) the Luminous Mysteries

4. When they saw the angels in the sky at Christmas, the shepherds were
(a) dancing (b) eating breakfast (c) getting ready for church (d) watching over their flocks

5. When Jesus was born, the king of Judea was a mean man named
(a) Herod (b) Pilot (c) Judas (d) Herbert

6. When the angel came to tell Mary she would bear a son named Jesus, Mary was engaged to a man named
(a) Gabriel (b) Joseph (c) Zachary (d) Joshua

7. The sign in the sky that led the wise men to Jesus was
(a) a full moon (b) an eclipse of the sun
(c) a star in the East (d) a huge, white cloud

8. Starting on the first Sunday of Advent, many families and parishes light candles
(a) to pray for world peace (b) on an Advent wreath (c) in front of statues of St. Patrick
(d) to save on electricity

9. The words the shepherds heard the angels sing to announce Jesus' birth were
(a) "Glory to God in the highest" (b) "This is the Lamb of God" (c) "Hosanna in the highest" (d) "We three kings of orient are"

10. Jesus' cousin was born six months before Jesus. This cousin's name was
(a) Simon Peter (b) John the Baptist
(c) James, the son of Zebedee (d) Thomas

11. Jesus was born in
(a) Bethlehem (b) Jerusalem (c) Damascus
(d) Corinth

12. The name of the angel who came to announce Jesus' birth to Mary was
(a) Michael (b) Gabriel (c) Raphael (d) Moroni

13. The inspiration for Santa Claus comes from
(a) St. Claude Columbiere (b) *Sinterklaas*
(c) Nicodemus (d) St. Nicholas of Myra

14. The wise men brought Jesus gifts of gold, frankincense, and
(a) myrrh (b) a silver spoon and cup (c) toys
(d) almonds

15. "Did you not know that I must be in my Father's house?" were Jesus' words
(a) when he was dying on the cross
(b) to Joseph and Mary when they found him in the Temple when he was twelve years old
(c) when he said Peter would have the keys of the kingdom (d) when he told the disciples he would give them a new commandment

Pflaum Publishing Group, Dayton, Ohio 45439 (800-543-4383) www.pflaum.com Permission is granted by the publisher to reproduce this page for noncommercial use only.

1. (a) *Christmas* comes directly from the Old English phrase, *Christ's Mass*.

2. (c) Bethlehem was crowded because the emperor had ordered people to register in their hometowns. There wasn't any room in the inn so Mary and Joseph stayed in a stable and laid Jesus in a manger, a food box for animals. That's how humble the birthplace of Jesus was.

3. (a) The Joyful Mysteries are the Annunciation, the Visitation, the Nativity, the Presentation in the Temple, and the Finding of Jesus in the Temple.

4. (d) The shepherds were so frightened by the sight of the angels that they needed to be told, "Do not be afraid." Later they went to see Jesus.

5. (a) Herod was the king of Judea when Jesus was born. He did not like the fact that the wise men were seeking "the child who was born king of the Jews." (Matthew 2:2)

6. (b) Joseph was the man Mary was engaged to marry. He was a carpenter.

7. (c) The wise men saw a star in the East and followed it a great distance to find Jesus.

8. (b) Advent wreaths have three purple candles and one pink one. The circle of the wreath and the evergreens often used to make the wreath remind us of God's everlasting love.

9. (a) See Luke 2:14. We use these words at Mass when we pray the Gloria. Many parts of the Mass are taken from the Bible.

10. (b) John the Baptist was the son of Mary's cousin Elizabeth and her husband Zachary. When the angel told Mary that Elizabeth was expecting a baby, Mary hurried to Elizabeth's house to help until John was born.

11. (a) Although they lived in Nazareth, Mary and Joseph had to register in Bethlehem, the city of David, because Joseph was descended from the family of David. It was while they were there that Jesus was born.

12. (b) Luke 1:26 gives us the angel's name. In Christian art Gabriel is often shown offering Mary a lily, which is the symbol of her purity.

13. (d) St. Nicholas, the Bishop of Myra in the fourth century, is the patron saint of children, sailors, and brides.

14. (a) See Matthew 2:11. Myrrh was an expensive ointment.

15. (b) When he was twelve, Jesus was separated from his parents for three days. His parents found him in the Temple listening to the rabbis and teachers. When Mary and Joseph scolded him and told him they were worried, this is what he replied! See Luke 2: 49.

Advent-Christmas Quiz

1. The word for Christmas in French is
(a) *Noel* (b) *Baba Yaga* (c) *Sinterklaas*
(d) *Gesundheit*

2. We owe the beautiful Christmas carol "Silent Night" to
(a) Mozart (b) Beethoven (c) Brahms
(d) a broken pipe organ

3. A Jesse tree
(a) shows the family tree of Jesus who was descended from David, Jesse's son (b) is a tree David planted for his father (c) is the name for Christmas tree in Hebrew (d) none of these

4. On Epiphany we celebrate
(a) Moses and God's people passing through the Red Sea (b) Jesus rising from the dead
(c) the three kings seeing Jesus
(d) Jesus ascending into heaven

5. The custom of using *Xmas* for Christmas
(a) uses an abbreviation for Christ that was used early in the Church's history (b) has only been used in modern times (c) comes from Santa Claus (d) means crossing Christ out of Christmas

6. At Christmas there is usually a special celebration of Mass
(a) at midnight (b) at sunrise (c) at 2:00 p.m.
(d) at 3:00 p.m.

7. The wise men did not return to King Herod to tell him where the newborn king was because
(a) they were warned in a dream and went home another way (b) Joseph told them not to (c) Mary was suspicious of Herod (d) their camels were too tired

8. The Sunday between Christmas and New Year's is the feast of
(a) Pentecost (b) the Holy Family
(c) the Ascension (d) Holy Thursday

9. When Jesus was still a baby, Joseph and Mary took him all the way to Jerusalem to
(a) visit relatives (b) buy him new clothes
(c) present him in the Temple (d) show him the city

10. The number of Sundays in Advent is
(a) four (b) five (c) six (d) seven

11. Most of the songs we sing during the Christmas season are called
(a) sonatas (b) symphonies (c) carols
(d) ballads

12. When Mary visited her cousin Elizabeth, John the Baptist (still in Elizabeth's womb)
(a) leapt for joy at Mary's greeting (b) was born at once (c) kept very quiet (d) changed his name to Peter

13. At the Annunciation the Angel Gabriel greeted Mary with the famous words
(a) "Hosanna in the highest!" (b) "Hail, full of grace! The Lord is with you!" (c) "Go in peace to love and serve the Lord!" (d) "Lord, I am not worthy!"

14. After Jesus was born, King Herod
(a) went to find Jesus (b) sent rich gifts to Bethlehem (c) ordered his soldiers to kill all children in Bethlehem two years old or younger (d) ignored the whole thing

15. The Blessed Mother appeared to St. Juan Diego near Mexico City in 1531, and is honored as
(a) Our Lady of Guadalupe (b) Our Lady of Fatima (c) the Sorrowful Mother (d) the Madonna of the Mountains

7

flaum Publishing Group, Dayton, Ohio 45439 (800-543-4383) www.pflaum.com Permission is granted by the publisher to reproduce this page for noncommercial use only.

1. (a) *Noel* is the French word for Christmas, as in "The First Noel."

2. (d) We owe this carol to an Austrian priest and his organist. Because the church organ was broken, they were worried that their plans for music for Christmas Mass would be spoiled. So organist Franz Gruber set a poem of Father Josef Mohr's to music for guitar.

3. (a) The custom of using a Jesse tree to show Jesus' family tree comes from pictures that decorated early Bible manuscripts. Jesus was known as a son of David. The prophet Isaiah said, "A shoot shall come out from the stump of Jesse" (Isaiah 11:1), and this was taken to mean Jesus.

4. (c) The feast of the three kings, or Epiphany, is the day many people in other countries exchange their Christmas gifts. This is in honor of the three gifts the kings brought to Jesus—gold, frankincense, and myrrh.

5. (a) The *X*, which stands for the Greek letter *chi*, was used along with the Greek letter *rho*, as an early abbreviation for the word *Christ*. Far from crossing Christ out of Christmas, *Xmas* is part of our long history!

6. (a) Midnight Mass is usually very beautiful with lots of singing and candles.

7. (a) Matthew 2:12 tells us the three kings were warned in a dream not to return to Herod. This made Herod furious.

8. (b) The Sunday after Christmas is a natural time to celebrate the life of the Holy Family and to think about those hidden years of Jesus' life, when he was growing up in Nazareth.

9. (c) It was the custom among devout Jews to present their firstborn sons to the Lord in the Temple. Mary and Joseph offered a pair of turtledoves in sacrifice.

10. (a) The four Sundays in Advent are symbolized by the four candles on the Advent wreath. The first Sunday in Advent marks the beginning of a new Church year.

11. (c) The word *carol* comes from an Old English word that means "ring dance with song." It's important for families to learn and sing the traditional religious carols since singing carols is often not permitted in public schools.

12. (a) See Luke 1:41. Even though he was not born yet, John reacted to the presence of Mary and of Jesus in her womb.

13. (b) These first two sentences of the Hail Mary come from Luke 1:28. The next sentence of the prayer comes from Luke 1:42.

14. (c) King Herod was jealous because the wise men told him a new baby would be a king.

15. (a) Our Lady of Guadalupe is patroness of the Americas. Her image on St. Juan Diego's *tilma*, or cloak, can still be seen. It is on display in Mexico City. The feast of Our Lady of Guadalupe is December 12. St. Juan Diego's feast day is December 9.

1. When King Herod ordered his soldiers to kill the babies of Bethlehem, Joseph
(a) had a dream that told him to take the Holy Family to Egypt (b) hid Jesus in a basket in the river (c) protected Mary and Jesus by fighting the soldiers (d) returned to Nazareth

2. An Hispanic Christmas custom of acting out Joseph and Mary looking for an inn is called
(a) Hide and Seek (b) the First Noel (c) Las Posadas (d) Tiny Tim's Christmas

3. The name *Emmanuel* means
(a) "Holy God, we praise thy name" (b) "Savior of the Universe" (c) "God is with us" (d) "Hark, the herald angels sing"

4. When an angel told Elizabeth's husband Zachary that he was going to be the father of John the Baptist,
(a) Zachary went to visit St. Joseph (b) he knelt down and prayed in thanksgiving (c) he didn't believe the angel and was struck mute for nine months (d) he passed out gifts

5. The custom of having a Nativity scene at Christmas began
(a) with Francis of Assisi (b) in England (c) at a cave in Nazareth (d) with a modern greeting-card company

6. An important belief of Christianity—the teaching that the Son of God became man and was born of the Virgin Mary—is called
(a) infinity (b) the Incarnation (c) Extreme Unction (d) the Intercessions

7. The Immaculate Conception
(a) means that Mary was preserved from sin from the first moment of her conception in her mother's womb (b) means that Mary conceived Jesus by the power of the Holy Spirit (c) was proclaimed in the year 1215 AD (d) none of these

8. At the Visitation, Mary's cousin Elizabeth greeted her with these famous words
(a) "Alleluia! Christ is risen!" (b) "Hosanna in the highest!" (c) "Blessed are you among women, and blessed is the fruit of your womb!" (d) "Hail, holy queen, mother of mercy!"

9. The word the Bible uses for the wise men in the Christmas story is
(a) *Caesar Augustus* (b) *Magi* (c) *geniuses* (d) *scribes*

10. The word *Advent* means
(a) "the coming" (b) "the end" (c) "Christ's Mass" (d) "Epiphany"

11. The region of Palestine where the Holy Family made their home was called
(a) Jerusalem (b) Rome (c) Corinth (d) Galilee

12. When Joseph found out Mary was going to have a baby, his first reaction was
(a) joy (b) prayer (c) thanksgiving (d) he wanted to divorce her quietly

13. The only two Gospels that tell about the birth of Jesus are
(a) Matthew and Paul (b) Matthew and Luke (c) Peter and Paul (d) Peter and John

14. Before Jesus was born, Joseph and Mary needed to go to Bethlehem because
(a) Caesar Augustus wanted the whole empire to register in their familys' hometowns (b) Mary wanted to visit relatives (c) Joseph wanted to visit relatives (d) an angel told them in a dream to do this

15. When Joseph and Mary presented Jesus in the Temple as a baby, the two people who witnessed it were named
(a) Peter and Paul (b) Simeon and Anna (c) Simon and Jude (d) James and John

9

Pflaum Publishing Group, Dayton, Ohio 45439 (800-543-4383) www.pflaum.com Permission is granted by the publisher to reproduce this page for noncommercial use only.

1. (a) You can read about this in Matthew 2:13. The Holy Family stayed in Egypt until King Herod died.

2. (c) In this Hispanic tradition two people representing Joseph and Mary go from house to house looking for a "room in the inn." They are turned away until they reach the last house, at which a Christmas party has been arranged.

3. (c) See Matthew 1:23. By taking on human nature, the Second Person of the Trinity became "God-with-us" in a new way.

4. (c) See Luke 1:20. After John was born, Zachary could talk again and he sang a beautiful hymn of praise that the Church calls the "Benedictus." See Luke 1:68-79.

5. (a) In 1223, St. Francis arranged for the first Nativity scene. It was near the Italian town of Grecchio, from which we have the word *créche*.

6. (b) Jesus became one of us to accomplish the work of our salvation. He shared our human nature.

7. (a) Many people think the term *Immaculate Conception* refers to Jesus' being conceived in Mary's womb. Actually the term refers to Mary's conception in her mother Ann's womb. The doctrine of the Immaculate Conception was announced in 1854, and it tells us that Mary was given special gifts by God because of the role she was going to play in salvation history.

8. (c) This second line of the "Hail Mary" is found in Luke 1:42. The first line is from the Angel Gabriel's greeting at the Annunciation. See Luke 1:28. The phrase "Holy Mary, Mother of God" was added in the Middle Ages.

9. (b) Though the Bible does not mention the wise men by name, the tradition has developed that their names were Gaspar, Melchior, and Balthasar. The idea that there were three of them comes from the fact that three gifts are mentioned: gold, frankincense, and myrrh. See Matthew 2:11.

10. (a) The word is borrowed directly from a Latin word meaning "the coming." Advent is the liturgical season in which we wait for "the coming" of the birth of Jesus.

11. (d) Galilee was the region of Palestine where the little town of Nazareth was located. It was far from Jerusalem, which was a major city.

12. (d) You can read about this in Matthew 1:19-22. Joseph was so upset he needed to have an angel come to him in a dream to tell him what to do.

13. (b) Only Matthew and Luke wrote about the Christmas story. Neither Peter nor Paul wrote Gospels, though they did write epistles, or letters.

14. (a) The emperor Caesar Augustus wanted to have everyone register for purposes of collecting taxes and raising an army. It was difficult for Mary to travel so near her time of giving birth. Bethlehem was about seven miles from Nazareth, a long journey at the time.

15. (b) Simeon and Anna were elderly people who had been faithfully praying for the Messiah to come. Simeon's words have become the Night Prayer of the Church, "Master, now you are dismissing your servant in peace." (Luke 2:29)

Bible Quiz

1. There are two main parts of the Bible, the Old Testament and the
(a) Book of Genesis (b) Book of Proverbs
(c) Book of Daniel (d) New Testament

2. God promised Noah to never again destroy the earth by flood. The sign of God's promise is
(a) the rainbow (b) the daisy (c) the rose
(d) incense

3. The Old Testament leader who made the walls of Jericho fall down
(a) Jeremiah (b) Joshua (c) King David
(d) King Saul

4. Jesus was baptized in
(a) the River Jordan (b) the Nile
(c) the Mississippi (d) the Red Sea

5. King David
(a) was just a boy when he killed Goliath
(b) played the harp and sang songs to God
(c) was king for 40 years (d) all of these

6. In an Old Testament story, a young woman told her mother-in-law Naomi, "Where you go, I will go." The young woman's name was
(a) Ruth (b) Jezebel (c) Sarah (d) Elizabeth

7. The garden where Adam and Eve lived before disobeying God was called
(a) Zion (b) Jerusalem (c) Eden (d) Nazareth

8. At the miracle of the multiplication of the loaves and fishes
(a) a little boy offered Jesus five barley loaves and two fish (b) Jesus changed water into wine (c) Jesus healed ten lepers (d) Jesus cured the blind man of Jericho

9. The beautiful Old Testament queen who saved the Jewish people from being killed was Queen
(a) Priscilla (b) Sarah (c) Esther (d) Rachel

10. Moses
(a) was a baby left in a basket in the reeds along the river bank (b) heard God speaking to him from a burning bush (c) told Pharaoh of Egypt, "Let my people go!" (d) all of these

11. The names of the four Gospel writers are Matthew, Mark, Luke, and
(a) John (b) Peter (c) Paul (d) Bartholomew

12. The Old Testament prophet who spent some time in a lions' den was
(a) Elijah (b) Jeremiah (c) Daniel (d) John the Baptist

13. Jesus' hometown was
(a) Nazareth in Galilee (b) Jerusalem
(c) Bethlehem (d) Jericho

14. The animals came onto Noah's ark
(a) on tiptoe (b) two by two (c) in animal crates
(d) on motorcycles

15. Belief in angels
(a) is not a truth of our faith (b) is a truth of our faith that is based on what we read in the Bible (c) is not taught by other churches (d) none of these

Pflaum Publishing Group, Dayton, Ohio 45439 (800-543-4383) www.pflaum.com Permission is granted by the publisher to reproduce this page for noncommercial use only.

Bible Rookie Quiz Answers

1. (d) Old Testament books make up about three-fourths of the Bible; New Testament books make up the other fourth.

2. (a) See Genesis 9:8-17 to read the story. Whenever we see a rainbow, we are reminded of God's promise.

3. (b) Joshua had his troops march around the walls of the city seven times, with the priests blowing their horns at the same time. When the priests gave a long blast on their horns, the people shouted, and the walls came tumbling down. See Joshua 6:15-20.

4. (a) Jesus was baptized by John the Baptist in the River Jordan. When Jesus stepped out of the water, the Holy Spirit descended on him like a dove, and a voice from heaven said, "You are my son, the Beloved; with you I am well pleased." (Mark 1:9-11)

5. (d) King David was a powerful king who united his kingdom. Before he died, David made sure that his son Solomon would be the next king. Solomon became known for his wisdom. See 1 Kings 3:16-28.

6. (a) Songs based on Ruth's words are often used at weddings. See Ruth 1:16-17. Ruth and Naomi were both poor widows. They went back to Bethlehem together after their husbands died. There Ruth married Boaz. She became the great-grandmother of King David and was an ancestor of Jesus.

7. (c) After Adam and Eve were cast out of the Garden of Eden, God placed an angel at the entrance, guarding it with a flaming sword. See Genesis 3:23-24.

8. (a) Andrew brought the five barley loaves and two fish to Jesus, but the apostles privately said, "What are they among so many people?" After the miracle, thousands were fed and twelve baskets of food were left over. See John 6:1-13.

9. (c) The Book of Esther tells the story of how the beautiful Queen Esther steps in when Haman, an evil official of the king, plots to have all the Jews killed. She saves the Jews, and it is Haman who is killed.

10. (d) Read Exodus 2:1-22 to learn about Moses' early life. He went on to receive the Ten Commandments from God and to lead the chosen people to the land God promised them.

11. (a) John is the writer of the Fourth Gospel. The word *Gospel* means "good news."

12. (c) This story is told in Daniel 6:10-23. The king of Babylon put Daniel in the lions' den because he wouldn't worship a false god. God saved Daniel from the jaws of the lions.

13. (a) We learn that Jesus, Mary, and Joseph lived in Nazareth where Jesus "increased in wisdom and age." (Luke 2:52) We know very little about this time of Jesus' life except that he learned to be a carpenter, probably from Joseph.

14. (b) You can read the story of Noah's ark in chapters 6-9 of the Book of Genesis.

15. (b) Belief in angels is a truth of our faith. We read about angels in the Bible. The Angel Gabriel tells Mary that she will have a son named Jesus (Luke 1:26-32). The Archangel Michael fights against evil (Revelation 12:7-8). The Archangel Raphael reveals himself to Tobit and his son Tobias (Tobit 12:14-15). The Church honors Gabriel, Michael, and Raphael on their feast day, September 29.

Bible Quiz

1. The first miracle of Jesus was
(a) feeding five thousand people with five barley loaves and two fish (b) healing the blind man of Jericho (c) changing water into wine at the wedding in Cana (d) calming the storm at sea

2. The great leader of the chosen people who received the Ten Commandments from God was
(a) Abraham (b) King David (c) Moses (d) Zerubbabel

3. The writer of most of the letters in the New Testament was
(a) St. Peter (b) St. Paul (c) St. Bartholomew (d) St. Nicholas

4. Jesus taught his disciples by telling short stories called
(a) parables (b) riddles (c) fables (d) parentheses

5. Of the following, the one who was not one of the original twelve apostles is
(a) John (b) Judas Iscariot (c) Paul (d) Andrew

6. The first book of the Old Testament is the Book of
(a) Revelation (b) Acts of the Apostles (c) Jeremiah (d) Genesis

7. Jesus said, "Where two or three are gathered in my name...." The rest of this statement is
(a) "I am there among them" (b) "they must sell all, give to the poor, and come follow me" (c) "the kingdom of heaven is theirs" (d) "they shall inherit the earth"

8. A special promise between God and God's people is called a
(a) truce (b) covenant (c) treaty (d) deal

9. The friend Jesus raised from the dead after four days was
(a) Lazarus (b) Timothy (c) Barnabas (d) Jonah

10. Jesus' name in Hebrew is
(a) James (b) Joshua (c) Zebedee (d) John

11. The "bread from heaven" that God provided for Moses and the Israelites as they journeyed in the desert for forty years was called
(a) manna (b) matzo (c) challah (d) unleavened

12. Jesus said, "Do this in remembrance of me"
(a) at the Last Supper (b) when he was on the cross (c) when he healed the lepers (d) just before he ascended into heaven

13. The Holy Spirit came down upon Mary and the disciples
(a) in Bethlehem (b) at Pentecost (c) while Jesus was standing in their midst (d) in a rowboat on the Sea of Galilee

14. The saint who baptized the Lord was
(a) St. Simon the Zealot (b) St. John the Baptist (c) St. James (d) St. Peter

15. Most of the Old Testament was originally written in
(a) English (b) Polish (c) French (d) Hebrew

13

flaum Publishing Group, Dayton, Ohio 45439 (800-543-4383) www.pflaum.com Permission is granted by the publisher to reproduce this page for noncommercial use only.

Bible Almost-Expert Quiz Answers

1. (c) At the wedding feast in Cana, Mary asked Jesus to help the bride and groom who had run out of wine for their guests. He changed water into wine so delicious that some guests said the bridal couple had saved the best wine for last. See John 2:1-11.

2. (c) Moses was born in Egypt and adopted by Pharaoh's daughter. God called him to lead the chosen people out of Egypt to the promised land. Abraham and King David are familiar names, but there actually was a Zerubbabel. See if you can find his name in the family history of Jesus in Matthew 1:1-17.

3. (b) There are 21 letters in the New Testament, and St. Paul wrote 13 of them. Saints Peter, John, James, and Jude are others who wrote New Testament letters.

4. (a) Jesus used many parables to emphasize his points. Two are the parable of the prodigal son (Luke 15:11-32) and the parable of the good Samaritan (Luke 10:25-37).

5. (c) Paul was not one of the original twelve apostles, but he had such a powerful experience of the risen Jesus that Paul became a great missionary during the years of the early Church. See Acts 9:1-19.

6. (d) Genesis tells the stories of Adam and Eve, Noah, Abraham, and Jacob and his twelve sons.

7. (a) This statement is found in Matthew 18:20. It is used to encourage us to gather together to pray. Praying in private is a good thing, of course, but we also need to pray with others.

8. (b) In the Old Testament, there are many examples of God's covenant—with Abraham (Genesis 17:1-9), with Noah (Genesis 9:8-16), and with Moses (Deuteronomy 5, 6, and 7). In these covenants, God promises to be faithful to his people, and they promise to be faithful to him. In the New Testament Jesus establishes a new covenant by laying down his life for all people (1 Corinthians 11:25).

9. (a) The story of the raising of Lazarus is told in John 11:1-44. Lazarus was the brother of Martha and Mary of Bethany, and Jesus visited their home often.

10. (b) *Jesus* is the Latin form of the Greek translation of the Hebrew name *Joshua*. It means "God saves."

11. (a) Manna "was like coriander seed, white, and the taste of it was like wafers made with honey." (Exodus 16:31) To learn more about this amazing "bread from heaven," read Exodus 16.

12. (a) At his Last Supper with the apostles, when Jesus instituted the Eucharist, he said, "Do this in remembrance of me." (Luke 22:19) The priest repeats this statement at every Mass.

13. (b) The story of the Holy Spirit's coming at Pentecost is told in Acts 2:1-17. We learn that three thousand people were baptized that day.

14. (b) St. John the Baptist was Jesus' cousin. When Jesus was baptized, a voice came from heaven and said, "This is my Son, the Beloved, with whom I am well pleased." (Matthew 3:17)

15. (d) The Old Testament was written through a long period of time in Hebrew.

Bible Quiz

1. St. John the Baptist died
(a) in a sword fight (b) of pneumonia (c) by having his head cut off (d) in a chariot accident

2. When we are talking about the Bible, the word *evangelist* means
(a) a Gospel writer (b) anyone who is baptized (c) someone who gave his or her life for the faith (d) an early pope

3. At Pentecost the Holy Spirit appeared over the heads of disciples
(a) as a ladder going up to heaven (b) as the right hand of God (c) as a halo over each person (d) as tongues of fire

4. Jews call the first five books of the Old Testament
(a) the Torah (b) the New Testament (c) the Acts of the Apostles (d) the Gospels

5. The scholarly Doctor of the Church who single-handedly translated the Bible into Latin is
(a) St. Peter (b) St. Francis Xavier (c) St. Columba (d) St. Jerome

6. When Jesus was twelve years old
(a) he got separated from his parents in Jerusalem (b) Mary and Joseph had to search anxiously for him for three days (c) he sat among the rabbis in the Temple (d) all of these

7. A Gentile is
(a) anyone who is not a Jew (b) anyone who is an orthodox Jew (c) one of the twelve tribes of Israel (d) a Jewish high priest

8. In the Book of Exodus we learn that the ark of the covenant
(a) was a portable golden box carried on poles (b) contained the tablets of the law, the rod of Aaron, and a sample of manna (c) was honored as a symbol of God's presence (d) all of these

9. The religious order that preserved the Bible during the Dark Ages by writing out copies by hand is
(a) the Benedictines (b) the Franciscans (c) the Dominicans (d) the Jesuits

10. When Moses came down the mountain after receiving the Ten Commandments from God, he found the chosen people
(a) worshiping the one true God (b) dancing around a golden calf (c) playing a game (d) sleeping

11. The language Jesus spoke was
(a) English (b) French (c) Aramaic (d) German

12. A religion that does not honor the Old Testament as the word of God is
(a) Christianity (b) Judaism (c) Islam (d) Buddhism

13. The Gospel writer who also wrote the Acts of the Apostles was
(a) Matthew (b) Luke (c) Nathaniel (d) Timothy

14. The prophet Elijah
(a) challenged the wicked Queen Jezebel (b) challenged the 400 prophets of Baal on Mt. Carmel (c) ascended into heaven in a fiery chariot (d) all of these

15. The one Gospel that is very different from the other three is the Gospel of
(a) Peter (b) John (c) James (d) Matthew

flaum Publishing Group, Dayton, Ohio 45439 (800-543-4383) www.pflaum.com Permission is granted by the publisher to reproduce this page for noncommercial use only.

Bible Scholar Quiz
Answers

1. (c) You can read about John the Baptist's death in Matthew 14:3-12. Herod was so delighted with Salome's dancing at his birthday party that he promised her anything she wanted. She asked Herod for John the Baptist's head on a platter.

2. (a) The word *evangelist* comes from a Greek word that means "one who announces the good news." The four evangelists, or Gospel writers, are Matthew, Mark, Luke, and John.

3. (d) Acts 2:3 describes how tongues of fire rested on each of the apostles. Then, filled with the Holy Spirit, they began to speak in the native languages of the Jews from every nation who were living in Jerusalem.

4. (a) The word *Torah* simply means "the teaching" and refers to the teachings of Moses.

5. (d) St. Jerome (345-420) was from Italy but eventually moved to Bethlehem where he could concentrate on translating the Bible into the language of the people of his day, Latin. There is a famous legend that he removed a thorn from a lion's paw and tamed the lion. St. Jerome tells us, "We must translate the words of Scripture into the deeds of life."

6. (d) You can read this story in Luke 2:41-52. As you can imagine, Mary and Joseph were very worried about Jesus. They did not completely understand Jesus' explanation for his absence. So Mary "treasured all these things in her heart," trying to understand what Jesus' words meant.

7. (a) *Gentile* is the word for anyone who is not a Jew. It was used this way in our Lord's time, and it is still used this way today.

8. (d) From the time when the Jews wandered in the desert until the fall of Jerusalem, the ark of the covenant was honored. After that, it disappeared, but legend says that the prophet Jeremiah hid it on Mt. Nebo. See 2 Maccabees 2:4-8.

9. (a) From the sixth century onward, St. Benedict's monks carefully made copies of the Bible and other books. The other three religious orders were not formed until the twelfth century or later.

10. (b) The Israelites thought Moses was taking too long with God on the mountain so they made a golden calf to worship. When he saw what the people had done, Moses was so angry he broke the stone tablets. He went up the mountain a second time to ask God for two more stone tablets.

11. (c) Aramaic was the language of the people who lived in Palestine during our Lord's time.

12. (d) Judaism, Christianity, and Islam all look to Abraham as the "father" of their faith and honor most of the same Old Testament Scriptures. Buddhism is based on the teachings of the Buddha, Siddhartha Gautama. *Buddha* means the "enlightened one."

13. (b) The books of Luke and Acts are meant to be read one after another. The Acts of the Apostles picks up where the Gospel of Luke leaves off.

14. (d) Elijah's story is told in 1 Kings 17-21. He was perhaps the fieriest of God's prophets. His is definitely an action story.

15. (b) Peter and James were not Gospel writers. The Gospels of Matthew, Mark, and Luke tell many of the same stories about Jesus. The Gospel of John, which was written much later, is very different from the other three. John's Gospel focuses on Jesus' revelation of God's plan of salvation.

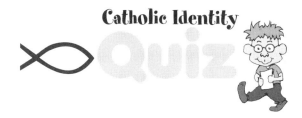

Catholic Identity Quiz

1. The holy table at which the priest celebrates Mass is called
(a) the sacristy (b) the altar (c) the vestibule (d) the cornerstone

2. The sign that the Blessed Sacrament is present in the tabernacle in church is
(a) a burning sanctuary lamp (b) flowers (c) candlesticks (d) statues

3. A person who genuflects
(a) kneels on the kneeler in the pew (b) dips a hand in holy water (c) bends the right knee to the floor and rises again (d) gets baptized on Holy Saturday

4. A priest who leads a parish is called
(a) a pastor (b) a monk (c) a pope (d) a nun

5. The teaching that there are three persons in one God is called
(a) the Messiah (b) the Resurrection (c) the Ascension (d) the Trinity

6. The ending of the Mass prayer, "Lord, I am not worthy to receive you" is
(a) "but only say the word and I shall be healed" (b) "Holy, Holy, Holy, Lord God of power and might" (c) "Peace be with you" (d) "Go in peace to love and serve the Lord"

7. We call the part of the Mass when we stand up and express our belief in God
(a) Communion (b) the collection (c) Lamb of God (d) the Profession of Faith

8. Before the Second Vatican Council, Mass all around the world was celebrated in
(a) German (b) French (c) Latin (d) English

9. The Church's sacrament of forgiveness is called
(a) the sacrament of Reconciliation (b) the sacrament of Penance (c) Confession (d) all of these

10. At Mass the cup containing the precious Blood of Christ is called
(a) a chalice (b) a vestment (c) a cruet (d) an alb

11. A person using a rosary is
(a) kneeling on it (b) praying with it (c) wearing it (d) smelling it

12. "Bless us, O Lord, and these your gifts" is the beginning of
(a) the Apostles' Creed (b) grace before meals (c) the Lord's Prayer (d) the guardian angel prayer

13. On an altar in church or in a chapel, a tabernacle contains
(a) clothing worn by the priest during Mass (b) bells (c) the Blessed Sacrament (d) incense

14. If you find a lost object, the Church teaches that
(a) you should leave it where you found it (b) the rule is finders keepers (c) you should try to return it to the owner if possible (d) you should give it to the poor

15. The Our Father was taught to the disciples by
(a) the Blessed Mother (b) St. Joseph (c) the prophet Isaiah (d) Jesus

Pflaum Publishing Group, Dayton, Ohio 45439 (800-543-4383) www.pflaum.com Permission is granted by the publisher to reproduce this page for noncommercial use only.

1. (b) The altar is consecrated, or blessed, setting it aside for use in liturgies. An altar that is fixed to the floor often has an inlaid altar stone that contains a relic of a saint. A relic is part of the physical remains of a saint or an object closely associated with a saint, as in pieces of clothing.

2. (a) The lamp kept burning to indicate the presence of the Blessed Sacrament is called the sanctuary lamp. The sanctuary is the place in the church where the priest, servers, and other ministers perform their functions. It is usually set off from the rest of the church in some way—a raised floor, special shape, or special decoration.

3. (c) When we enter the presence of the Blessed Sacrament, we genuflect or bow before we enter our pew as a sign of reverence to the Lord.

4. (a) The word *pastor* comes from a Latin word that means "shepherd," or "one who tends and feeds a flock." A pastor is a priest entrusted with the care of a parish.

5. (d) The central mystery of our faith is the Most Holy Trinity. This teaching is called a mystery because, on our own, we couldn't understand how one God is Father, Son, and Holy Spirit. We know about the Trinity through the revelation of God. We remind ourselves of the Holy Trinity each time we make the Sign of the Cross and say, "In the name of the Father, and of the Son, and of the Holy Spirit."

6. (a) This prayer is said just after the Lamb of God and before we receive Communion. It comes from what the centurion said when Jesus offered to go to the centurion's house to heal his servant. See Matthew 8:8.

7. (d) The creed most often used in the Profession of Faith at Sunday Masses is called the Nicene Creed. The Apostles' Creed is another expression of our faith.

8. (c) Before the Second Vatican Council (1962-1965), the priest celebrated Mass in Latin.

9. (d) This is one sacrament with many names and graces. In most parishes the schedule includes weekly opportunities to receive the sacrament of Penance. Many parishes also celebrate the sacrament in penance services once or twice a year, commonly in Advent and Lent.

10. (a) The cup is called a chalice. Receiving the Body and Blood of Jesus in both forms, or species, is recommended as a fuller sign of Communion. However, anyone who receives either the consecrated bread or the consecrated wine receives Jesus' Body and Blood.

11. (b) The rosary has been a popular way of praying since the Middle Ages. There are twenty mysteries of Our Lord's life to think about as we pray the Our Fathers and Hail Marys on the rosary beads.

12. (b) The rest of this traditional prayer is: "which we are about to receive from your goodness, through Christ, our Lord. Amen."

13. (c) Usually fashioned of gold with beautiful craftsmanship, the tabernacle holds consecrated hosts for veneration and for taking to those who are sick.

14. (c) The *Catechism of the Catholic Church* tells us that deliberately keeping a lost object when you know its owner is a sin against the seventh commandment, "You shall not steal."

15. (d) When Jesus' disciples asked him to teach them to pray, he taught them this prayer. See Luke 11:1-4.

Catholic Identify Quiz

1. Another name for a sermon is
(a) *hominy* (b) *homily* (c) *Extreme Unction*
(d) *Eucharistic Prayer*

2. A martyr is a person who
(a) dies for the faith (b) teaches the faith
(c) goes out into the desert to live a solitary life
(d) lives in a monastery

3. The word used by the Church to mean God's call to the priesthood or religious life is
(a) *concelebration* (b) *vocation* (c) *invocation*
(d) *community*

4. The person who leads parishioners in song at Mass is called a
(a) cantor (b) altar server (c) bishop (d) pope

5. In Holy Communion, Jesus is really and truly present
(a) only in the consecrated hosts (b) only in the consecrated wine (c) in both species, the bread and the wine (d) only as a symbol

6. All these actions are sins against the eighth commandment except for
(a) gossiping (b) lying (c) stealing (d) speaking falsely under oath

7. In the sacrament of Reconciliation, the action of the priest as he says the words forgiving your sins is called
(a) absolution (b) blessing (c) anointing (d) chrism

8. When a bishop comes to your parish, you can tell who he is because
(a) he wears a tall hat in the procession
(b) he walks barefoot (c) he's the one leading the choir (d) he's always the shortest one in the procession

9. The Hebrew word *shalom* means
(a) "faith" (b) "hope" (c) "charity" (d) "peace"

10. Ancient underground Christian cemeteries are known as
(a) catechisms (b) catacombs (c) caterpillars
(d) cat-o-nine-tails

11. The holy oil used for Confirmation is called
(a) liniment (b) oleo (c) chrism (d) glycerin

12. The year that the Mass began to be said in English in this country was
(a) 1492 (b) 1776 (c) 1964 (d) 2003

13. The house where nuns live is called a
(a) convent (b) shrine (c) cathedral (d) rectory

14. The seal of the confessional means
(a) a priest sponsors a seal at the zoo (b) a priest can never ever reveal a person's sins (c) a priest must make the Sign of the Cross when you confess your sins (d) you must make the Sign of the Cross when you confess your sins

15. The day the Holy Spirit came upon the disciples and Mary in the upper room is called
(a) Ordinary Time (b) Advent (c) Lent
(d) Pentecost

19

flaum Publishing Group, Dayton, Ohio 45439 (800-543-4383) www.pflaum.com Permission is granted by the publisher to reproduce this page for noncommercial use only.

1. (b) The homily is the part of the Mass in which the priest relates the Scripture readings to our daily lives. The word *homily* comes from a Greek word meaning "to have a conversation with."

2. (a) Before Christianity was legalized in 313, many Christians gave up their lives for their faith. They were martyred by being thrown to lions or by being crucified or beheaded. Even in modern times, Christians sometimes give up their lives to uphold their faith. Archbishop Oscar Romero is called the martyr of San Salvador. Because he spoke out for the poor who were oppressed in his country, he was killed in 1980 as he celebrated Mass.

3. (b) The word *vocation* comes directly from the Latin word that means "to call." Young people are encouraged to listen carefully for what God calls them to do with their lives.

4. (a) The word *cantor* comes from the word that means "to sing" in Latin. It's important for all the people to join in the singing at Mass. St. Augustine said that the person who sings prays twice!

5. (c) Jesus is truly present in both species of the Eucharist, in the consecrated bread and in the consecrated wine.

6. (c) Stealing is a sin against the seventh commandment: "You shall not steal." The other actions are sins against the eighth commandment: "You shall not bear false witness against your neighbor."

7. (a) The word *absolution* comes from two Latin words that together mean "to free from." In the sacrament of Reconciliation, the priest, in the name of Christ and his Church, frees you from your sins.

8. (a) For ceremonial occasions, the bishop wears a miter, a tall hat with two bands of material that sometimes hang from the back. A bishop is given the care of a diocese, a certain geographic area of the Church. One of a bishop's many duties is to be the "ordinary" minister of Confirmation. This means that it is a bishop who usually celebrates the sacrament of Confirmation. He can delegate his role to another priest, especially the pastor of the parish in which Confirmation is being celebrated.

9. (d) The word *shalom*, which means "peace," is both a greeting and a prayer all by itself. It is used as a wish for God's peace.

10. (b) As the tombs of martyrs became places to be honored, Mass was often celebrated in the underground burial grounds, or catacombs, where these tombs were located.

11. (c) The words *chrism* and *Christ* both come from Greek words that have to do with anointing. *Christ* comes from the Greek word *Christos*, which means the "anointed one." *Chrism* comes from the Greek word *chrisma* and refers to the oil the Church uses for anointing in Baptism, Confirmation, and Holy Orders.

12. (c) Mass was once celebrated in Latin all aroundthe world. At the Second Vatican Council, which was held from 1962-1965, the council fathers agreed that Mass should be said in the vernacular, the language of each country.

13. (a) Not all nuns live in convents these days, but many do. A rectory is the house for parish priests.

14. (b) Every priest who hears confessions must keep those sins absolutely secret. St. John Nepomucene (1340-1393) was tortured and executed when he refused to tell an angry king the sins the queen had confessed.

15. (d) Pentecost, which comes from a Greek word meaning "fifty," is celebrated fifty days after Easter. Pentecost is often called the birthday of the Church because this is when the disciples received the full strength of the Holy Spirit and began spreading the good news of Jesus Christ to the world.

Catholic Identity Quiz

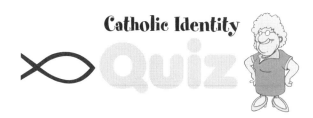

1. In the early days of the Church, hermits were people who
(a) gave the popes advice (b) elected the bishops (c) went out into the desert to live a life of prayer (d) crowned the kings who were Catholic

2. Most older churches are built
(a) in the shape of a cross (b) in a circular shape (c) in the shape of a triangle (d) with spiral staircases

3. The artist who painted the ceiling of the Sistine Chapel in the Vatican is
(a) Edward Steichen (b) Gus Sistine (c) Michelangelo (d) Sandro Botticelli

4. Pride, greed, lust, anger, gluttony, envy, and sloth are
(a) the seven "deadly" sins (b) original sin (c) the corporal works of mercy (d) the spiritual works of mercy

5. Our Pope's name is
(a) John Paul II (b) Benedict XIV (c) Benedict XVI (d) none of these

6. Regarding occult practices (such as witchcraft, Ouija boards, horoscopes, and the like), the Church
(a) takes a neutral position (b) warns the faithful strongly against them (c) says they're not against the Ten Commandments (d) none of these

7. The Second Vatican Council took place in
(a) the 1760s (b) the 1860s (c) the 1960s (d) the early 2000s

8. The belief that Mary, at the end of her life, was taken up to heaven body and soul is called
(a) the Assumption (b) the Visitation (c) sanctifying grace (d) Holy Orders

9. Catechists are
(a) underground burial chambers of the early Church (b) those who teach the faith (c) those preparing to be baptized (d) categories of sins

10. A miter is
(a) a tall hat worn by a bishop (b) a tall spire on a steeple (c) a corporal work of mercy (d) a very small sin

11. Feeding the hungry, clothing the naked, visiting the sick, and the like, are known as the
(a) spiritual works of mercy (b) corporal works of mercy (c) marks of the Church (d) Ten Commandments

12. Using a fish as a symbol of Christ
(a) dates from the early days of Christianity (b) was a secret way early Christians showed other believers that they were Christian (c) was used because the Greek word for fish formed an abbreviation of Jesus' titles (d) all of these

13. Of the following, the one thing not necessary for a good confession is
(a) sorrow for your sin (b) confession of the sin to a priest (c) confession of the sin to the person offended (d) penance done, as given by the priest

14. The split between Protestants and Catholics in the 1500s is called
(a) the Reformation (b) the Western Schism (c) ecumenism (d) none of these

15. In Christian art, icons are
(a) mazes (b) modern pictures of the crucifixion (c) sacred representations of Jesus, Mary, or the saints used in Eastern churches (d) always mosaics

Pflaum Publishing Group, Dayton, Ohio 45439 (800-543-4383) www.pflaum.com Permission is granted by the publisher to reproduce this page for noncommercial use only.

1. (c) After Christianity was legalized in 313, it became more difficult for Christians to maintain their early fervor, so people tried to get away from the "world" by going out to desert places to pray.

2. (a) If you look carefully at the shape of older churches, you'll see that they have the long part of a cross (called a nave) and two sidebars (called transepts). Since the Second Vatican Council, many churches have been built with other shapes.

3. (c) Michelangelo (1475-1564) painted the ceiling of the Sistine Chapel at the request of Pope Julius II.

4. (a) These sins are also called the "capital" sins. They are considered to be at the root of all other sins.

5. (c) Pope Benedict XVI was consecrated pope on April 19, 2005. He is the 265th successor to Peter and is originally from Germany.

6. (b) The Church firmly opposes all occult practices, saying they are against the first commandment and that they are the opposite of putting ourselves confidently into God's hands concerning the future.

7. (c) The Second Vatican Council (1962-1965) had a major impact on the Church as we know it today.

8. (a) Mary's Assumption into heaven is not found in the Bible, but from the very early days of the Church, this belief was evident. Pope Pius XII officially proclaimed the Assumption a truth of faith in 1950. The feast of Mary's Assumption is celebrated on August 15, and is a holy day of obligation in some parts of the world, including the United States.

9. (b) The word *catechist* comes from a Greek word meaning "echo." Catechists have echoed the faith to their students through the ages.

10. (a) A miter is two pieces of stiff triangular-shaped material attached at the sides to form a hat. Israelite priests used to wear something similar and, in about the twelfth century, the miter became the customary hat for Catholic bishops.

11. (b) *Corporal* means "bodily." The corporal works of mercy are those acts that tend to a person's bodily needs. Six of the seven traditional corporal works of mercy are found in Matthew 25:34-40. The seventh, burying the dead, was added at a later time.

12. (d) The Greek word for "fish" is *ichthys*, which is a proclamation about Jesus, formed by the first letters of the Greek words for "Jesus Christ, Son of God, is Savior."

13. (c) It is not required to confess the sin to the person offended. However, in cases of stolen goods, the sinner must make amends wherever possible.

14. (a) The Protestant Reformation is normally dated from 1517, when Martin Luther, an Augustinian monk, made a series of statements about abuses in the Church. There was other unrest in the Church before this time.

15. (c) Icons are images painted on walls or flat panels, using rich colors, often backed with gold. Sometimes they are made of mosaics. Eastern churches use icons rather than statues in their churches. Icons are becoming popular for personal prayer use in the West.

Commandments-Beatitudes Quiz

1. The Golden Rule is "Do to others...
(a) as you would have them do to you" (b) as they have already done to you" (c) as they have done to others" (d) none of these

2. We begin most of our prayers by saying, "In the name of the Father, and of the Son, and of ...
(a) the saints" (b) the angels" (c) the Holy Spirit" (d) the Blessed Mother"

3. Christians celebrate the Lord's Day on
(a) Monday (b) Wednesday (c) Thursday (d) Sunday

4. The Ten Commandments given by God show us
(a) how to have true worship and morality (b) how to grab the best for ourselves (c) how to do enough to get by (d) none of these

5. The number of commandments given by God to Moses is
(a) three (b) five (c) ten (d) twelve

6. The eight statements in Matthew's Gospel that describe a person who is blessed in the eyes of God are called
(a) Holy Orders (b) the gifts of the Holy Spirit (c) the Beatitudes (d) Pentecost

7. "Turn the other cheek" is a famous saying of Jesus that means we shouldn't
(a) fight (b) steal (c) lie (d) genuflect

8. In order for an action to be a sin
(a) you must get caught at it (b) it must be done on purpose (c) it must be an accident (d) someone must dare you to do it

9. The first murderer in the Bible was
(a) Cain (b) Jacob (c) Herod (d) Judas

10. The commandments God gave to Moses were written on
(a) yellow paper (b) two tablets of stone (c) a scroll (d) sand

11. Jesus taught the Beatitudes to
(a) Peter, James, and John (b) the twelve apostles (c) his disciples (d) Mary and Joseph

12. The usual place for Catholics to gather on Sundays is
(a) the mall (b) the ballpark (c) their parish church (d) the town square

13. Jesus told his followers to "love your neighbor as...
(a) yourself" (b) your country" (c) your pets" (d) your toys"

14. "It is more blessed to give than ...
(a) to receive" (b) to have two tunics" (c) to shop" (d) to want more things"

15. On Sunday, the Lord's Day, all Catholics are supposed to
(a) go to Mass (b) rest from unnecessary work (c) visit the sick and the elderly (d) all of these

23

flaum Publishing Group, Dayton, Ohio 45439 (800-543-4383) www.pflaum.com Permission is granted by the publisher to reproduce this page for noncommercial use only.

Commandments-Beatitudes Rookie Quiz

1. (a) This famous saying of Jesus is from his teaching called the Sermon on the Mount. See Luke 6:31.

2. (c) The words of the Sign of the Cross honor the Holy Trinity and strengthen us in our work and prayer.

3. (d) Christians celebrate the Lord's Day on Sunday because that's the day Jesus rose from the dead.

4. (a) The commandments are a sign of the covenant, or solemn agreement, that God made with his chosen people. God promised to take care of his people and they promised to follow God's commandments.

5. (c) When God spoke with Moses on Mount Sinai, he gave Moses Ten Commandments for all of Israel to observe. You can read the commandments in Deuteronomy 5:1-21.

6. (c) You can read the Beatitudes in Mathew 5:3-12. In the Beatitudes, Jesus teaches us how to be happy and challenges us to be our best.

7. (a) This saying comes from Matthew 5:38-39. Jesus' followers would have been familiar with the old law that Jesus is quoting. You can read it in Leviticus 24:19. But he's bringing them a new law, urging his followers to be peacemakers.

8. (b) Even if you don't get caught, actions against the commandments are sins. But something that happens by accident is not a sin.

9. (a) Cain and Abel were the sons of Adam and Eve. Cain murdered his brother Abel out of anger and jealousy. See Genesis 4:3-8.

10. (b) The Bible tells us that the commandments were written on stone tablets by the finger of God. See Exodus 31:18.

11. (c) In Matthew 5:1, we read that Jesus gave the Beatitudes to his disciples. *Disciple* is a word that means "student" and is used to describe those who hear and listen to the teaching of Jesus, not only in New Testament times, but in all ages.

12. (c) When Catholics gather in their parishes on Sundays to celebrate Mass, they are obeying the third commandment: "Remember to keep holy the LORD'S Day."

13. (a) "Love your neighbor as yourself" is the second part of what Jesus tells us is the greatest commandment. The first part is, "You shall love the Lord your God with all your heart, and with all your soul, and with all your mind." (Matthew 22:36-39)

14. (a) St. Paul quotes these words of Jesus to tell us how to respond to those who need our help. See Acts 20:35.

15. (d) Sunday is a day to grow closer to God.

Commandments-Beatitudes Quiz

1. Jesus told his disciples that the greatest commandment is
(a) do not steal (b) do not be greedy (c) do not lie
(d) none of these

2. The mountain where God gave Moses the Ten Commandments is
(a) Mt. Sinai (b) Mt. Ararat (c) Mt. Everest
(d) Mt. Zion

3. "You shall not kill" is the
(a) third commandment (b) fifth commandment
(c) seventh commandment (d) ninth commandment

4. The fourth commandment seems to be only about children and parents, but it actually asks us to respect
(a) all older people (b) teachers (c) leaders
(d) all of these

5. "You shall not covet your neighbor's goods" is
(a) the third commandment (b) the fourth commandment (c) the eighth commandment
(d) the tenth commandment

6. The first word of all the Beatitudes is
(a) *Blessed* (b) *Wise* (c) *Chosen* (d) *Glorious*

7. "You shall not covet your neighbor's wife" is the
(a) third commandment (b) fifth commandment
(c) seventh commandment (d) ninth commandment

8. Part of being "pure of heart" is being modest, which means
(a) choosing appropriate clothing (b) resisting unhealthy curiosity (c) avoiding inappropriate advertisements and TV shows (d) all of these

9. "Blessed are the peacemakers...
(a) for they will be called children of God"
(b) for they shall get rich" (c) for they shall be powerful on earth" (d) for they shall be comforted"

10. "Blessed are the merciful..."
(a) for the Bible says "an eye for an eye and a tooth for a tooth" (b) for they will receive mercy (c) for all eyes are upon them (d) for they are not good examples

11. "You shall not steal" is the
(a) first commandment (b) third commandment
(c) fifth commandment (d) seventh commandment

12. The improper use of God's name is against the
(a) second commandment (b) third commandment
(c) sixth commandment (d) tenth commandment

13. "You shall not commit adultery" is the
(a) second commandment (b) fourth commandment (c) sixth commandment (d) eighth commandment

14. It is against the eighth commandment
(a) to lie (b) to destroy the reputation of another person (c) to be sarcastic at the expense of another (d) all of these

15. "Remember to keep holy the LORD'S Day" is the
(a) first commandment (b) third commandment
(c) seventh commandment
(d) tenth commandment

©flaum Publishing Group, Dayton, Ohio 45439 (800-543-4383) www.pflaum.com Permission is granted by the publisher to reproduce this page for noncommercial use only.

1. (d) Jesus tells us the greatest commandment is, "You shall love the Lord your God with all your heart, and with all your soul, and with all your mind. This is the greatest and first commandment. And a second is like it: You shall love your neighbor as yourself." (Matthew 22:36-39)

2. (a) Mt. Sinai is the name of the mountain. See Exodus, chapters 19 and 20. Another name for the mountain is Mt. Horeb.

3. (b) The fifth commandment forbids direct and intentional killing. Every human life is sacred because it was created by God.

4. (d) Obeying the fourth commandment brings peace, especially when parents and leaders are mindful of God's law.

5. (d) This commandment forbids greediness, which is the root of stealing and jealousy.

6. (a) Our word *Beatitude* comes from the Latin word for "blessed" or "happy." It is only an accident that the word can also be read as *Be-attitudes*, but these are truly attitudes for being. You can read the Beatitudes in Matthew 5:3-10 and Luke 6:21-23.

7. (d) This commandment forbids desiring the spouse of another. It urges us to be pure at heart.

8. (d) The virtue of modesty protects the inner person as well as the outer person. It helps us to control our actions, dress, and conversation.

9. (a) This is one of the Beatitudes that Jesus gave us. See Matthew 5:9. We are never too young to learn to be peacemakers.

10. (b) See Matthew 5:7. How does the message of this Beatitude compare with this part of the Lord's Prayer: "and forgive us our trespasses as we forgive those who trespass against us"?

11. (d) This is the seventh commandment. It asks us to respect the property of other people as well as to respect all of creation.

12. (a) Taking the "name of the LORD your God in vain" extends to the improper use of Jesus' name and of the names of Mary and the saints.

13. (c) This is the sixth commandment. It forbids sins against chastity, which is a healthy, holy attitude toward sexuality. To be chaste is to accept our sexuality as a gift from God to be used wisely according to our state in life—married or single.

14. (d) The eighth commandment is concerned with truth, the basic building block of society. Lying hurts the liar and the person lied about. The lie has effects on others as well. Gossiping and spreading rumors are related to lying.

15. (b) This is the third commandment. The "LORD'S Day" is Sunday, when the Lord rose from the dead. It is our duty to celebrate and worship God by participating in Mass on Sunday. This duty is rooted in God's love for us.

Commandments-Beatitudes Quiz

1. Jesus said, "Truly I tell you, just as you did it to one of the least of these who are members of my family...
(a) you did it to me" (b) it brings honor to the whole human race" (c) it will earn you points in heaven" (d) you do for yourself"

2. "You shall not bear false witness against your neighbor" is the
(a) second commandment (b) fourth commandment (c) sixth commandment (d) the eighth commandment

3. "Honor your father and your mother" is the
(a) second commandment (b) third commandment (c) fourth commandment (d) fifth commandment

4. A word used in the Bible to mean "wanting strongly, without regard to the rights of others" is
(a) *trivet* (b) *trivial* (c) *covet* (d) *civil*

5. The seventh commandment forbids
(a) shoplifting (b) vandalism (c) cheating (d) all of these

6. "I am the LORD your God: you shall not have strange gods before me" is the
(a) first commandment (b) sixth commandment (c) seventh commandment (d) tenth commandment

7. "You shall not take the name of the LORD your God in vain" is the
(a) first commandment (b) second commandment (c) fourth commandment (d) eighth commandment

8. Jesus gave his disciples the Beatitudes
(a) from the cross on Calvary (b) at the Ascension (c) in the Sermon on the Mount (d) when he cured the ten lepers

9. Besides killing, the fifth commandment forbids
(a) deep anger (b) hatred (c) fighting (d) all of these

10. "Blessed are those who mourn...
(a) for they shall love their enemies" (b) for they will be comforted" (c) for they do not hide their light under a bushel" (d) for they are peacemakers"

11. Swearing a false oath is
(a) rejecting the Pledge of Allegiance to the flag (b) a sin against the second commandment (c) intending to keep a promise (d) saying the Boy Scout Oath or the Girl Scout Promise and Law

12. "Blessed are the meek...
(a) for others will notice them" (b) for they will pray harder" (c) for they shall inherit the earth" (d) all of these

13. Experimenting with the occult (Ouija boards, fortunetelling, horoscopes) is forbidden by the
(a) first commandment (b) fourth commandment (c) fifth commandment (d) eighth commandment

14. Adultery is
(a) being an adult (b) lying (c) a sin forbidden by the sixth commandment (d) getting a divorce

15. *Blasphemy* means
(a) speaking or acting against God (b) blowing up a building with dynamite (c) being sly (d) having a good time at a party

Pflaum Publishing Group, Dayton, Ohio 45439 (800-543-4383) www.pflaum.com Permission is granted by the publisher to reproduce this page for noncommercial use only.

Commandments-Beatitudes Scholar Quiz
Answers

1. (a) In Matthew 25:35-46, Jesus tells his followers that, whenever they met the needs of others, they did these things to him. And in the same way, whenever they failed to meet the needs of others, they did these things to him.

2. (d) The eighth commandment forbids all offenses against truthfulness.

3. (c) The Gospels tell us that even Jesus was obedient to his parents, Mary and Joseph. See Luke 2:51.

4. (c) To covet means to want something so much that you are willing to commit a sin to get it. Coveting is a sin against both the ninth and tenth commandments.

5. (d) The seventh commandment also forbids cheating on taxes, fraud in business dealings, and not doing your best at work or school. It urges us to use the gifts of creation well.

6. (a) This is the first commandment, which tells us to worship only the one true God.

7. (b) This is the second commandment. Because the name of God is holy, we need always to respect it. This commandment also calls us to respect the names of Jesus, Mary, and all the saints.

8. (c) In Matthew 5:1, we read that Jesus "went up the mountain; and after he sat down, his disciples came to him. Then he began to speak, and taught them...." Chapters 5-7 of Matthew's Gospel contain the Beatitudes and many other teachings of Jesus.

9. (d) Jesus taught that the fifth commandment includes anger, fighting, and insults. You can read Jesus' teaching in Matthew 5:21-24.

10. (b) See Matthew 5:4. Christians experience sorrow when they see that something or someone is standing in the way of building the kingdom of God. Mourning the victims of tragedy and injustice helps Christians to realize the brokenness of life and experience the personal call to change.

11. (b) Taking an oath, or swearing, is taking God as a witness to what you are saying. This involves using God's name. A false oath calls on God to be a witness to a lie.

12. (c) See Matthew 5:5. In this Beatitude, Jesus challenges us to identify with and work to help the poor, the oppressed, the outcast, and the powerless.

13. (a) All of these practices are attempts to know and control the future, which is in the hands of God alone.

14. (c) In marriage the husband and wife promise to be faithful to each other. Adultery breaks that promise and is a serious sin.

15. (a) Because blasphemy is contrary to the respect due God and his name, it is a sin against the second commandment.

Lent-Easter Quiz

1. Lent lasts
(a) thirty days (b) forty days (c) fifty days
(d) sixty days

2. Simon of Cyrene was the man who
(a) helped Jesus carry his cross (b) ran away when
Jesus was praying in the garden (c) waited outside
the courtyard when Pontius Pilate judged Jesus
(d) held the rooster that crowed three times

**3. Jesus said, "This is my body" and "This is
my blood" to the apostles**
(a) at the wedding feast in Cana (b) at Zacchaeus'
house (c) at the Last Supper (d) when he fed five
thousand people with five loaves and two fishes

**4. The mysteries of the rosary that include
Jesus' suffering and death are**
(a) the Joyful Mysteries (b) the Sorrowful Mysteries
(c) the Glorious Mysteries (d) the Luminous
Mysteries

5. Peter denied Jesus
(a) three times (b) four times (c) ten times
(d) seventy times seven times

6. Lent is a time for an extra effort in
(a) fasting (b) giving to the poor (c) prayer
(d) all of these

**7. "Today you will be with me in Paradise,"
is a promise Jesus gave to**
(a) the good thicf (b) Mary his mother (c) John his
beloved disciple (d) Peter

**8. The Sunday before Easter we listen to a
very long Gospel and carry**
(a) statues (b) palms (c) holy water (d) umbrellas

9. Calvary is the name of the hill where
(a) Jesus was crucified (b) Jesus prayed in the garden (c) Moses received the Ten Commandments
(d) the shepherds watched their flocks at
Christmas

**10. When Pontius Pilate asked the people
what he should do with Jesus, they shouted**
(a) "Let him go!" (b) "Send him to Rome!"
(c) "Crucify him!" (d) "Let him be a soldier!"

**11. The man who offered his new tomb for
Jesus to be buried in was**
(a) Peter (b) Thomas (c) Judas Iscariot
(d) Joseph of Arimathea

12. Lent officially begins on
(a) Ash Wednesday (b) Holy Thursday
(c) Good Friday (d) New Year's Day

**13. The apostle who betrayed Jesus with a
kiss was**
(a) Doubting Thomas (b) Nathaniel (c) Judas
Iscariot (d) James

**14. "Father, into your hands I commend my
spirit," were Jesus' words as**
(a) he died on the cross (b) he prayed in the garden (c) he carried the cross (d) he was crowned
with thorns

**15. Our special celebration of the
Resurrection of Jesus is on**
(a) the Ascension (b) Christmas (c) Easter
(d) Pentecost

laum Publishing Group, Dayton, Ohio 45439 (800-543-4383) www.pflaum.com Permission is granted by the publisher to reproduce this page for noncommercial use only.

Answers

1. (b) Not counting Sundays, Lent lasts forty days. Officially the three days from Holy Thursday to Easter are called the *Triduum*, the holiest days of the year. It is especially important to go to church on these days.

2. (a) When Jesus was carrying the cross, the soldiers made Simon help Jesus. See Mark 15:21.

3. (c) It was at the Last Supper that Jesus instituted the Eucharist. On Holy Thursday we celebrate this in a special way at the Mass of the Lord's Supper.

4. (b) The Sorrowful Mysteries are: the Agony of Christ in the Garden, the Scourging of Jesus, the Crowning with Thorns, the Carrying of the Cross, and the Crucifixion of Jesus.

5. (a) All four Gospel writers tell about Peter's denial of Jesus. After he realized what he'd done, he wept bitterly. See Matthew 26:69-75, Mark 14:66-72, Luke 22:54-62, and John 18:15-18, 25-27.

6. (d) Fasting, giving to the poor (also called "almsgiving"), and prayer are traditional practices all year long, but are especially stressed during Lent. If you give up something like candy or soft drinks for Lent, give the money you save to the poor.

7. (a) The good thief scolded the other thief for mocking Jesus. Then he asked, "Jesus, remember me when you come into your kingdom." (Luke 23:43) Legend tells us that the good thief had a name, St. Dismas, and that he is the patron of all repentant thieves.

8. (b) On Palm Sunday, the Sunday before Easter, we remember the day when Jesus entered Jerusalem riding on a donkey with everyone waving palms and shouting "Hosanna!" See Matthew 21:1-11. We also remember that this was followed by the events that led to his death on a cross. We read about these sad events in the part of the Gospels that is called the Passion. See Mark 14:1-15:47.

9. (a) Jesus was crucified on Calvary between two thieves. *Calvary* is the Latin translation of *Golgotha*, which means "place of the skull." Calvary was the place outside of Jerusalem where criminals were usually executed.

10. (c) Pontius Pilate didn't think Jesus was guilty, but he was afraid of the crowd. He took a bowl of water and washed his hands saying, "I am innocent of this man's blood." (Matthew 27:24)

11. (d) Joseph of Arimathea was a distinguished member of the Jewish council. He did not vote against Jesus the way most of the others did. It took great courage for him to go ask Pontius Pilate for Jesus' body.

12. (a) On Ash Wednesday we begin Lent by receiving ashes on our foreheads. This reminds us that we are mortal and that the whole season of Lent is one of repentance.

13. (c) The story of the betrayal of Jesus is found in Matthew 26:47-56. In Matthew 27:1-10, we learn that the chief priests of the Temple paid Judas thirty pieces of silver to betray Jesus.

14. (a) These were among Jesus' last words on the cross. We can use them as a prayer ourselves whenever we are troubled or afraid.

15. (c) Easter Sunday is the holiest day of the year, which is why Christians celebrate "the Lord's Day" every Sunday.

Lent-Easter Quiz

1. The color of the priest's vestments during Lent is
(a) black (b) green (c) violet (d) white

2. During Lent many parishes remember Jesus' passion and death by praying a popular devotion called
(a) the Stations of the Cross (b) the Nativity
(c) Pentecost (d) the Joyful Mysteries of the rosary

3. To betray Jesus, the chief priests of the Temple paid Judas Iscariot
(a) ten pieces of silver (b) thirty pieces of silver
(c) a hundred gold coins (d) nothing

4. Jesus' tunic was woven in one piece without any seams, so when he was crucified the soldiers
(a) rolled dice to see who would get it (b) ripped it so everyone would get a piece (c) raffled it off to the highest bidder (d) gave it to Jesus' mother

5. After Jesus died on the cross, a soldier pierced his side with a lance and
(a) nothing happened (b) water and blood flowed out (c) the soldier said, "This man deserved to die" (d) the soldier said, "I'm sorry I have to do this"

6. Some of Jesus' last words on the cross include
(a) "I am thirsty" (b) "Father, forgive them; for they do not know what they are doing" (c) "My God, my God, why have you forsaken me?" (d) all of these

7. On Palm Sunday the people of Jerusalem greeted Jesus with the words
(a) "Glory to God in the highest heaven, and on earth peace among those whom he favors"
(b) "Hosanna! Blessed is the one who comes in the name of the Lord!" (c) "Lord, I am not worthy" (d) "My Lord and my God"

8. We receive ashes on Ash Wednesday
(a) as a sign of penance (b) to remind us that one day we will die (c) to remind us to repent and believe in the Gospel (d) all of these

9. The oldest Christian feast is
(a) Easter (b) Thanksgiving (c) Fourth of July
(d) All Saints Day

10. The Bible says that when Jesus died
(a) there was an earthquake (b) the curtain of the Temple was torn in two (c) darkness came over the whole land (d) all of these

11. We call the day when Jesus rose into heaven
(a) the Ascension (b) Pentecost
(c) the Resurrection (d) Christmas

12. When Jesus was praying for his Father's help in the garden before he was crucified, he said, "Father, if you are willing, remove this cup from me." But he finished this request by saying,
(a) "yet, not my will but yours be done"
(b) "Blessed are the merciful" (c) "Our Father, who art in heaven" (d) "Hail Mary, full of grace"

13. Before they crucified Jesus, the soldiers
(a) treated him with respect (b) scourged him and crowned him with thorns (c) left him untouched in solitary confinement (d) put him under house arrest

14. After Peter denied Jesus three times,
(a) a rooster crowed (b) he heard a train in the distance (c) he was scolded by another apostle (d) the Roman soldiers whipped him

15. The saint who was the first person at the tomb on Easter morning was
(a) St. Peter (b) St Thomas (c) St. Francis of Assisi (d) St. Mary Magdalene

31

flaum Publishing Group, Dayton, Ohio 45439 (800-543-4383) www.pflaum.com Permission is granted by the publisher to reproduce this page for noncommercial use only.

1. (c) The color violet reminds us that the forty days of Lent are a time of penance.

2. (a) This popular devotion traces Jesus' journey from his trial to Calvary. Crosses or images, usually on the walls of a church, mark the fourteen stations. People commonly walk from station to station to pray and reflect on each step in Jesus' passion and death. Stations can be prayed privately or as a group.

3. (b) You can read about this in Matthew 26:14-16. Judas later regretted betraying Jesus and tried to give the money back, but the chief priests wouldn't take it. See Matthew 27:3-8.

4. (a) Jesus' "seamless garment" has become a symbol of the dignity of human life from natural beginning to natural end. The symbol comes from the respect that even the Roman soldiers had for this basic garment. See John 19:23-25.

5. (b) Later, touching this wound in Jesus' side would convince doubting Thomas to believe in Jesus' Resurrection. See John 20:24-29. The blood and water are symbols of dying and rising with Christ through Baptism.

6. (d) All of these were Jesus' words from the cross. All of them are good for us to ponder.

7. (b) Jesus came into Jerusalem riding a donkey with the people shouting "Hosanna!" This Hebrew word means "Save us, we pray!" We hear this word during Mass, during the blessing of the palms, and during the Palm Sunday procession.

8. (d) Though most Catholics participate in Mass and receive ashes on this day, Ash Wednesday is not a holy day of obligation. The ashes are sacramentals, signs the Church uses to remind us to be open to God's love. Not only are the ashes a sign that reminds us of the need to reform our lives, they are also a sign that we are choosing to do penance during Lent.

9. (a) Easter is the oldest feast day. Jesus' followers began to gather and remember Jesus' teaching and the events of his life very soon after they happened. Christmas was not celebrated until much later.

10. (d) You can read the story of what happened when Jesus died in Matthew 27:45-56. The Roman soldiers guarding Jesus were terrified by these events. One of the centurions said, "Truly this man was God's Son!"

11. (a) This story is in Acts 1:6-12. Jesus rose into heaven in the sight of his disciples, telling them to wait for the coming of the Holy Spirit at Pentecost. We celebrate the Ascension forty days after Easter.

12. (a) Jesus' prayer in the garden was so intense that he sweated drops of blood. He had asked Peter, James, and John to stay awake and pray with him at this important time, but they all fell asleep. See Luke 22:39-46.

13. (b) The soldiers not only whipped Jesus and crowned him with thorns, they also mocked him and spit at him. See Matthew 27:27-31.

14. (a) Jesus warned Peter that, before the rooster crowed, Peter would deny he knew Jesus three times. Peter swore he would never deny Jesus. When Peter heard the rooster, he suddenly remembered Jesus' word and wept bitterly. See Matthew 26:69-75.

15. (d) In Luke 8:2, we learn that Jesus cast out seven demons that had possessed Mary Magdalene. She became a faithful follower of Jesus. She stood at the cross with Jesus' mother (John 19:25), was the first to visit the tomb after the sabbath (John 20:1-2), and was the first to see the resurrected Jesus (John 20:11-18).

Lent-Easter Quiz

1. The Jewish religious ceremony Jesus and his disciples were celebrating at the Last Supper was
(a) Hanukkah (b) Yom Kippur (c) Passover (d) Christmas

2. People who have been studying all year to become Catholic are received into the Church
(a) at the Easter Vigil on Holy Saturday evening (b) at the Mass of the Last Supper on Holy Thursday (c) on Good Friday (d) during the procession on Palm Sunday

3. The initials _INRI_ above Jesus' head on a crucifix
(a) stand for "In the name of Rome, I salute you"
(b) stand for "Jesus of Nazareth, King of the Jews"
(c) were used for every crucified criminal
(d) none of these

4. The ashes used on Ash Wednesday come from
(a) the Holy Land (b) Rome (c) the palms from previous years' Palm Sundays (d) the bishop's fireplace

5. The word _Eucharist_ comes from a Greek word that means
(a) hope (b) charity (c) banquet (d) thanksgiving

6. The apostle who swore that he'd never deny Jesus even if everyone else did was
(a) Peter (b) Judas Iscariot (c) James (d) John

7. Between the Ascension and Pentecost, the disciples and Mary prayed
(a) in an upstairs room (b) at Mary's house (c) in the Temple (d) in the cave at Bethlehem

8. The difference between a cross and a crucifix is that
(a) a cross is always shaped like a capital "T"
(b) a crucifix always has an image of Jesus' body on it (c) a crucifix is always made of wood
(d) a crucifix is always made of precious metal

9. On Easter morning Mary Magdalene
(a) went to Jesus' tomb early in the morning
(b) brought oils and spices to anoint the body
(c) saw that the stone was rolled back from the tomb (d) all of these

10. When the chief priests would do nothing after Judas told them that he had betrayed an innocent man, Judas
(a) went to Pontius Pilate (b) hanged himself
(c) told the apostles about it (d) prayed in the Temple

11. Before he was betrayed and arrested, Jesus prayed in Gethsemane, a garden
(a) at the foot of the Mount of Olives (b) in Calvary
(c) in Bethlehem (d) in Nazareth

12. The word _alms_ means
(a) money and goods for the poor (b) meat that you don't eat during Lent (c) giving up candy
(d) saying extra prayers during Lent

13. A special ritual that happens on Holy Thursday evening at the Mass of the Lord's Supper is
(a) kissing the cross (b) blessing the Easter candle
(c) blessing the Easter water (d) the washing of the feet

14. Jesus instituted the Eucharist
(a) at the Last Supper (b) the night before he died
(c) using the bread and wine from the Passover meal (d) all of these

15. The only apostle left at the foot of the cross was
(a) St. John (b) St. Jude Thaddeus (c) St. Peter
(d) St. Antoninus

33

Pflaum Publishing Group, Dayton, Ohio 45439 (800-543-4383) www.pflaum.com Permission is granted by the publisher to reproduce this page for noncommercial use only.

Lent-Easter Scholar Quiz
Answers

1. (c) Jesus and the apostles were devout Jews, so they were celebrating Passover together. Passover reminds all Jews of their crossing over the Red Sea to escape slavery in Egypt.

2. (a) The Easter Vigil is a very special ceremony. The church is dark as the Easter candle is lighted. Then everyone lights a small candle, or taper, from the Easter candle. New Catholics are joyfully baptized, confirmed, and join with the rest of the community to receive the Eucharist for the first time.

3. (b) John's Gospel tells us that Pontius Pilate ordered this sign to be written on Jesus' cross in Latin, Greek, and Hebrew. See John 19:19-22. The letters *INRI* are the first letters of the words in the Latin translation.

4. (c) Some parishes mark the burning of the previous year's palms with a ceremony just before Lent begins.

5. (d) The Eucharist is the sacrament of the Body and Blood of Jesus Christ and is the central celebration of the Church's life.

6. (a) Peter was insistent that he'd never deny Jesus, yet he denied Jesus three times.

7. (a) After the Ascension the disciples missed Jesus and didn't know what was going to happen. They stayed together in what is often called the "upper room." Another name for this room is *cenacle*, which is a Latin word. In this room the Last Supper was celebrated, the resurrected Jesus appeared to the apostles, and the Holy Spirit descended to the apostles.

8. (b) A crucifix is a cross that has an image of Christ's body. This image is either of the suffering Savior or the risen Lord. The powerful symbol of the crucifix inspires us to remember the passion, death, and Resurrection of Jesus.

9. (d) Mary Magdalene ran to tell the news to Peter and John. When she returned later, Jesus appeared to her and told her that he was ascending to his Father. See John 20:1-2 and John 20:11-18.

10. (b) Judas tried to undo what he had done, but it was too late. He threw the thirty pieces of silver on the floor and then hanged himself. The chief priests could not put this blood money back into the treasury so they used the silver to buy a field for the burial of foreigners. See Matthew 27:3-10.

11. (a) Luke tells us that Jesus prayed so hard before his suffering and death that "his sweat became like great drops of blood falling down on the ground." (Luke 22:42-44)

12. (a) Alms are money or goods for the poor. We are supposed to be generous to the poor at all times, but Lent reminds us of this obligation in a special way.

13. (d) At the Mass of the Lord's Supper, the priest washes the feet of twelve parishioners just as Jesus washed the feet of his disciples at the Last Supper. This is to remind us to serve one another. See John 13:1-17.

14. (d) If you listen carefully at Mass, you can hear all of these facts mentioned in the prayers. We remember Jesus' gift of himself in the Eucharist at every Mass.

15. (a) John, often called "the one whom Jesus loved," was the only apostle to stand by Jesus to the end. All the others ran away. From the cross Jesus entrusted his mother to John's care. See John 19:26-27.

Sacraments Quiz

1. When there is a wedding in the Catholic Church, the sacrament celebrated is called
(a) Holy Orders (b) Confirmation (c) Matrimony
(d) Reconciliation

2. When we go into church, we make the Sign of the Cross with water from the holy water font
(a) to remind us of our Baptism (b) to wash our face (c) to wake ourselves up (d) because everyone else is doing it

3. When we receive Communion, the Eucharistic minister says, "Body of Christ" or "Blood of Christ." We respond by saying
(a) "Holy, Holy, Holy" (b) "Amen" (c) "Hosanna"
(d) "Alleluia"

4. Holy Orders is a sacrament for
(a) nuns (b) priests, bishops, and deacons
(c) laypeople (d) all of these

5. After we have told our sins to the priest in Confession, we need to say
(a) a good Act of Contrition (b) the Apostles' Creed (c) the Guardian Angel prayer (d) grace before meals

6. The "Holy Family" is
(a) Jacob and his twelve sons (b) James, John, and the Zebedee family (c) Jesus, Mary, and Joseph
(d) Peter and his wife and mother-in-law

7. At Mass, just before we receive Communion, we call Jesus the
(a) King of Kings (b) Lamb of God (c) Lion of Judah
(d) Alpha and Omega

8. The water for Baptism
(a) must come from a spring (b) comes from Vatican City where the Pope lives (c) is ordinary water that is blessed by a special prayer (d) has vitamins added

9. At Mass, the gifts that are brought forward to become the Body and Blood of Christ are
(a) bread and wine (b) water and wine (c) oil and water (d) candles and oil

10. Our Baptism makes us
(a) people who are mean to each other (b) people who don't need each other (c) members of the Church (d) none of these

11. A person going to Confession has the choice of being face-to-face with the priest or
(a) announcing his or her sins out loud to the church (b) writing a note (c) text messaging
(d) being behind a screen

12. To help them raise their newly baptized babies in the faith, parents choose
(a) godparents (b) good pediatricians (c) sports heroes (d) sponsors

13. We are baptized
(a) in the name of the Father only (b) in the name of the Son only (c) in the name of the Holy Spirit only (d) in the name of the Father, and of the Son, and of the Holy Spirit

14. In the Our Father, we pray "Forgive us our trespasses..."
(a) for we are not worthy to receive you" (b) as we forgive those who trespass against us" (c) and an eye for an eye and a tooth for a tooth" (d) for you are the Christ, the Son of God"

15. The person who said "I am the bread of life" was
(a) Peter (b) Thomas (c) Jesus (d) Bartholomew

flaum Publishing Group, Dayton, Ohio 45439 (800-543-4383) www.pflaum.com Permission is granted by the publisher to reproduce this page for noncommercial use only.

Sacraments Rookie Quiz Answers

1. (c) Matrimony is the name of the sacrament in which a man and a woman marry each other. A priest or a deacon witnesses the marriage in the name of the Church.

2. (a) The water reminds us of our Baptism, as does making the Sign of the Cross and saying, "In the name of the Father, and of the Son, and of the Holy Spirit."

3. (b) When we receive Communion, we bow our heads and then say "Amen" after the minister says "Body of Christ" and "Blood of Christ."

4. (b) Priests, bishops, and deacons become special ministers to serve the Church in the sacrament of Holy Orders.

5. (a) The Act of Contrition is also a good prayer to use for a night prayer before bed.

6. (c) Sometimes Jesus, Mary, and Joseph are also called the Holy Family of Nazareth. The Church has a special feast day to honor the Holy Family on the Sunday between Christmas and the Epiphany.

7. (b) We call Jesus the Lamb of God because he gave his life to save us from our sins.

8. (c) The water used for Baptism has received a special blessing, either just before the ceremony or at the Easter Vigil. In this blessing, the priest asks God to send the Holy Spirit upon the water so that the baptized can be born of water and the Spirit. Jesus told us that no one can enter the kingdom of God without being born of water and the Spirit. See John 3:5.

9. (a) In the Consecration at Mass, the gifts of bread and wine become the Body and Blood of Jesus Christ. Jesus becomes truly present in the consecrated bread and wine.

10. (c) Another name for the Church is the Body of Christ. This name helps us to see the unity of the Church. Jesus is the head and we are the members of the Body of Christ.

11. (d) The Church provides privacy for those confessing their sins. A priest may never ever reveal what you tell him in Confession.

12. (a) Parents, godparents, and all the members of the Church are expected to join in raising newly baptized infants in the faith.

13. (d) The priest or deacon says, "I baptize you in the name of the Father, and of the Son, and of the Holy Spirit" as a sign that, through Baptism, we share the life of the Most Holy Trinity.

14. (b) When we pray that God will forgive us in the same way we forgive others, we realize that we had better be quick to forgive!

15. (c) Jesus told his followers, "I am the bread of life. Whoever comes to me will never be hungry, and whoever believes in me will never be thirsty." (John 6:35) For the people of Jesus' time, who were very poor, this was reassuring. Jesus was telling them, and us, that he would always take care of those who believe in him.

Sacraments Quiz

1. When the priest sprinkles everyone at Mass with holy water, it reminds us of
(a) our Baptism (b) Holy Communion (c) Confirmation (d) rice being sprinkled at weddings

2. At the ordination of a priest, the visible sign of the sacrament of Holy Orders is
(a) everyone in church genuflecting at the same time (b) all the other priests concelebrating Mass (c) the laying on of hands by the bishop (d) the long procession into church

3. The sacrament of initiation that strengthens and completes the grace of Baptism is
(a) the Anointing of the Sick (b) Penance (c) Matrimony (d) Confirmation

4. When Jesus said, "What God has joined together, let no one separate," he was talking about the sacrament of
(a) the Anointing of the Sick (b) Holy Orders (c) Matrimony (d) Confirmation

5. In the sacrament of the Anointing of the Sick, the priest
(a) says special prayers and reads a Scripture passage (b) lays his hands on the heads of those to be anointed (c) anoints the foreheads and hands of the sick people (d) all of these

6. The power of the sacrament of Penance reconciles us
(a) to God (b) to the Church (c) with our neighbors (d) all of these

7. In case of emergency
(a) anyone can baptize a person (b) only a priest can baptize (c) only a sister can baptize (d) only a deacon can baptize

8. The newly baptized are given a candle lighted
(a) with their parents' wedding candle (b) from the Easter candle (c) with special matches (d) with two sticks rubbed together

9. Jesus said, "This is my body" and "This is my blood"
(a) at Cana in Galilee (b) at Bethlehem (c) at the Last Supper (d) while on the cross

10. After his Resurrection, Jesus told his apostles to
(a) go back to the slavery of Egypt (b) go and baptize all nations (c) let no one else become a member of the Body of Christ (d) teach no one else the things he had taught them

11. The sacrament of the Anointing of the Sick
(a) is not just for those in danger of death (b) may be received more than once (c) should be received before any serious operation (d) all of these

12. The word that means to "plunge or immerse in water" is
(a) *baptize* (b) *alphabetize* (c) *categorize* (d) *symbolize*

13. A special outpouring of the Holy Spirit on all the disciples happened
(a) on Epiphany when the three kings came (b) when Jesus got lost in the Temple (c) at Pentecost (d) at the Agony in the Garden

14. Water is poured over the baptismal candidate's head
(a) once (b) twice (c) three times (d) seventy times seven times

15. A Confirmation name is usually the name of
(a) a saint (b) a baseball star (c) a superhero (d) your place of birth

laum Publishing Group, Dayton, Ohio 45439 (800-543-4383) www.pflaum.com Permission is granted by the publisher to reproduce this page for noncommercial use only.

Sacraments Almost-Expert Quiz Answers

1. (a) The Rite of Sprinkling, as it is called, reminds us of our Baptism and of how our Baptism cleansed us from sin. This rite is often used at Masses during the Easter season.

2. (c) This sign means the new priest is consecrated, or set apart, for service to the Church.

3. (d) Baptism, Confirmation, and Eucharist are sacraments of initiation. Baptism is the beginning of new life in Christ, Confirmation is its strengthening, and the Eucharist nourishes us for growing in Christ.

4. (c) You can read Jesus' teaching about marriage in Matthew 19:3-6. In Ephesians 5:25-33, St. Paul compares the bond between a husband and wife to Christ's relationship to the Church.

5. (d) The final beautiful prayer of this sacrament is, "Through this holy anointing, may the Lord in his love and mercy help you with the grace of the Holy Spirit. May the Lord who frees you from sin save you and raise you up."

6. (d) The sacrament also brings us inner peace, reconciling us with ourselves.

7. (a) In case of emergency, anyone can baptize another person. There are only two requirements. First, the person baptizing must intend to do what the Church does in Baptism. Then the person must say, "I baptize you in the name of the Father, and of the Son, and of the Holy Spirit."

8. (b) The candle lighted from the Easter candle shows how close the newly baptized is to the Easter mystery and that from now on he or she is called to be "light of the world."

9. (c) Jesus said these words at the Last Supper when he instituted the Eucharist.

10. (b) Jesus said, "Go therefore and make disciples of all nations, baptizing them in the name of the Father and of the Son and of the Holy Spirit, and teaching them to observe everything that I have commanded you." (Matthew 28:19)

11. (d) At one time, the Anointing of the Sick was considered a sacrament for those close to death, and it came to be called "Extreme Unction." This understanding changed after the Second Vatican Council. Now the Church offers those who are about to die the Eucharist as *viaticum*, the spiritual food for their passing from this world to the Father.

12. (a) The Rite of Baptism includes immersing the candidate in water or pouring water over the head. This symbolizes the candidate's union with Christ's death from which the candidate rises again as a new creation.

13. (c) After the disciples received the Holy Spirit, they immediately began preaching and baptizing all who heard them. More than 3,000 were baptized on that day alone. You can read the whole story in Acts, chapter 2.

14. (c) The water is poured three times or the candidate is immersed three times to signify entering into the life of the Trinity.

15. (a) A Confirmation candidate usually chooses to take the name of a saint whose story he or she finds inspiring.

Sacraments Quiz

1. The sacrament intended to strengthen those who are seriously ill is
(a) described in the Letter of James (b) a community celebration (c) called the Anointing of the Sick (d) all of these

2. The Church requires engaged couples to prepare for marriage by going to
(a) law school (b) pre-Cana preparation (c) trade school (d) home economics classes

3. In the sacrament of Confirmation, candidates receive
(a) a white rose (b) a new white baptismal garment to replace the old one (c) a small votive candle (d) the mark, or seal, of the Holy Spirit

4. Seriously looking at the sins we have committed as we prepare for Confession is called
(a) absolution (b) an examination of conscience (c) making reparation (d) being truly sorry

5. The usual minister of the sacrament of Confirmation is
(a) a deacon (b) a priest (c) a bishop (d) the pope

6. The primary, or first, educators in the faith for children are
(a) their pastors (b) their parents (c) their catechists and religion teachers (d) EWTN (Eternal Word Television Network)

7. The newly baptized receive
(a) a white garment (b) a candle lighted from the Easter candle (c) a solemn blessing (d) all of these

8. Rosaries, medals, scapulars, and holy water are all
(a) sacramentals (b) pastorals (c) liturgies (d) sacristies

9. Holy chrism is
(a) oil to which balsam is added for fragrance (b) blessed during Holy Week at the Chrism Mass (c) used in Baptism, Confirmation, and Holy Orders (d) all of these

10. "What God has joined together, let no one separate" are Jesus' words about
(a) Holy Orders (b) Holy Communion (c) Matrimony (d) Confession

11. Of the following, the one that is not a gift of the Holy Spirit is
(a) courage (b) wisdom (c) right judgment (d) anger

12. The bread used for Holy Communion is usually unleavened to remind us of
(a) the unleavened bread the Jews ate in the haste of their escape from Egypt (b) the manna they ate while they wandered in the desert (c) the purity of Christ (d) all of these

13. "Be sealed with the Gift of the Holy Spirit" are the bishop's words as he anoints the foreheads of
(a) those confessing their sins (b) those receiving Communion (c) those being confirmed (d) those being married

14. The ministers of the sacrament of Matrimony are
(a) a priest and a deacon (b) the couple themselves (c) a priest and the Church community (d) a pastor and his associate

15. A Confirmation candidate chooses the help of a
(a) coach (b) deacon (c) sponsor (d) cheerleader

Pflaum Publishing Group, Dayton, Ohio 45439 (800-543-4383) www.pflaum.com Permission is granted by the publisher to reproduce this page for noncommercial use only.

Sacraments Scholar Quiz Answers

1. (d) In James 5:14-15, we see that, even in the earliest days, members of the Church prayed together and anointed the sick in the name of the Lord.

2. (b) Pre-Cana instructions and programs are named for the town of Cana, the site of the wedding where Jesus worked his first miracle—changing water into wine. You can read this story in John 2:1-11.

3. (d) Confirmation candidates receive the seal of Holy Spirit when they are anointed by the bishop. By this anointing, they receive the fullness of the Holy Spirit and are united more completely with the mission of Jesus. Because this is what happened to the apostles on Pentecost, we can say that the sacrament of Confirmation continues the grace of Pentecost in the Church.

4. (b) An examination of conscience can be done by examining our lives and actions against the Ten Commandments (Deuteronomy 5:6-21) or the Sermon on the Mount (Matthew 5-7).

5. (c) The bishop usually visits parishes to celebrate Confirmation, although he sometimes delegates this duty, especially to the pastor of a parish. At the Easter Vigil, the pastor confirms those who are being received into Church.

6. (b) The Church says that parents are the primary teachers of their children. At the same time, the Church promises to help parents with their responsibility. Priests, deacons, religious men and women, school principals, religion teachers, catechists—all have roles in educating children in their faith.

7. (d) The white garment symbolizes that the baptized person has "put on Christ." The candle signifies the person has received the light of Christ. The solemn blessing concludes the celebration of Baptism.

8. (a) Some sacramentals are objects, like blessed candles and palms, and some are actions, like blessings. Sacramentals prepare us to receive the grace of the sacraments.

9. (d) *Chrism* comes from a Greek word meaning "to anoint." The oil that is blessed at the Chrism Mass is distributed and used in all the parishes of a diocese.

10. (c) Jesus' strong words are part of his response to a question about divorce. See Matthew 19:3-9.

11. (d) The gifts of the Holy Spirit listed in the Rite of Confirmation are: wisdom, understanding, right judgment, courage, knowledge, reverence, and wonder and awe in the presence of God.

12. (d) When Moses led the chosen people out of Egypt, they were in such a hurry that they did not have time to use yeast to let their bread rise. They ate unleavened bread. See Exodus 12:33-34. The Jews remember this by celebrating the Passover each year. See Exodus 13:3-8.

13. (c) The bishop anoints the foreheads of the candidates with chrism by the laying on of his hand and pronounces these words.

14. (b) The spouses confer the sacrament of Matrimony by expressing their consent to marry. The priest or deacon who assists at the celebration receives the consent of the couple in the name of the Church and gives the Church's blessing.

15. (c) Often, to show the unity of Baptism and Confirmation, the Confirmation sponsor is one of the baptismal godparents.

Saints Quiz

1. St. Peter was
(a) a fisherman (b) a tentmaker (c) a weaver
(d) an electrician

2. St. Patrick is the patron saint of
(a) Italy (b) Ireland (c) Japan (d) Mexico

3. The patron saint for finding things that have been lost is
(a) St. Martin de Porres (b) St. Hedwig
(c) St. Anthony of Padua (d) St. Thomas Aquinas

4. The first Native American to be declared blessed (the step before becoming a saint) is
(a) Kateri Tekakwitha (b) Geronimo
(c) Chief Red Cloud (d) Apache Dan

5. The saint who followed what she called "The Little Way" to holiness is
(a) St. Augustine (b) St. Therese, the Little Flower
(c) St. John Bosco (d) St. Elizabeth of Hungary

6. The Aztec peasant who had a vision of Our Lady of Guadalupe in 1531 in Mexico is
(a) St. Juan Diego (b) St. Frances of Rome
(c) St. Lucy (d) St. Christopher

7. The saint who loved animals so much that animals are now blessed on his feast day is
(a) doubting Thomas (b) St. Francis of Assisi
(c) St. Bridget (d) St. Ignatius

8. The patron saint of France who cut her hair and dressed in armor to lead the army was
(a) St. Joan of Arc (b) St. Mary Magdalene
(c) St. Genevieve (d) St. Gertrude

9. Jesus' foster father St. Joseph was a
(a) bricklayer (b) shepherd (c) carpenter
(d) shoemaker

10. The woman whose home Jesus liked to visit and who is known as patron saint of cooks and homemakers is
(a) St. Agatha (b) St. Gabriel (c) St. Rose of Lima
(d) St. Martha

11. The saint who, according to legend, wiped the face of Jesus with her veil when he fell on his way to Golgotha is
(a) St. Veronica (b) St. Anne
(c) St. Catherine of Siena
(d) St. Elizabeth Ann Seton

12. The young man who traveled with St. Peter and wrote one of the Gospels is
(a) St. Nicodemus (b) St. Mark (c) St. Barnabas
(d) St. George

13. The founder of the religious order known as the Dominicans is
(a) St. Lawrence (b) St. Barbara (c) St. Cecelia
(d) St. Dominic

14. The first pope was
(a) St. Boniface (b) St. Andrew (c) St. Peter
(d) St. Luke

15. The Roman soldier-saint who cut his cloak in two and gave half to a beggar is
(a) St. Martin of Tours (b) St. Nicholas of Myra
(c) St. Paul Miki (d) St. Brendan the Navigator

Pflaum Publishing Group, Dayton, Ohio 45439 (800-543-4383) www.pflaum.com Permission is granted by the publisher to reproduce this page for noncommercial use only.

Saints Rookie Quiz

Answers

1. (a) St. Peter and his brother Andrew were both fishermen. Archaeologists think they've found the ruins of St. Peter's house in Capernaum. There is evidence that Peter's home was used as a church by the early Christians.

2. (b) St. Patrick (389-461) was kidnapped as a child and taken to Ireland as a slave. Later, after he escaped, he returned and preached the Gospel. He founded many churches and schools.

3. (c) St. Anthony (1195-1231) was famous in his day as a preacher. He is known to us as a helper in finding lost objects because he once prayed that a lost prayer book would be returned and it was.

4. (a) Blessed Kateri (1656-1680) was a young Mohawk girl when she became a Christian. Because of her faith, she was treated badly by her tribe and even her family. She eventually ran away from her tribe's home in upstate New York and joined a Native-American Christian colony near Montreal, Canada. She is known for her devotion to the Eucharist.

5. (b) The "Little Flower" (1873-1897) wrote that we should try to please God by doing even little things as sacrifices for his sake. She is the patron saint of the missions and her feast day is October 1.

6. (a) St. Juan Diego's vision took place in December. When the bishop asked for proof of Juan Diego's vision, Our Lady told Juan Diego where to find roses in December. He carried the roses to the bishop in his *tilma*, or cloak. When Juan Diego opened his tilma to show the roses to the bishop, there was a beautiful image of Our Lady on the inside of the cloak.

7. (b) St. Francis (1181-1226) is the patron saint of ecology, the science of caring for our whole planet. He was also famous as a peacemaker. He founded the Franciscans.

8. (a) St. Joan of Arc (1412- 431), the "Maid of Orleans," seemed to come out of nowhere to help the true king of France reclaim his throne. In war-torn France she made so many enemies that she was later accused of being a heretic and burned at the stake.

9. (c) In Matthew 13:55, when the people of Nazareth call Jesus the carpenter's son, we learn that St. Joseph was a carpenter. He must have taught Jesus the trade because in Mark 6:3, the people of Nazareth call Jesus the carpenter.

10. (d) St. Martha, her sister Mary, and brother Lazarus must have had a welcoming home. In the Bible we read accounts of Jesus' visits with them. See Luke 10:38-42 and John 12:1-3. There is also the story of how Jesus raised Lazarus from death. See John 11:1-44.

11. (a) Veronica's name means "true image." By stepping out of the crowd and helping a prisoner, she showed the true image of what a disciple should be.

12. (b) We don't know very much about St. Mark except that he is mentioned in Acts 12: 12, 25, and that his mother, Mary of Jerusalem, offered her house as a meeting place for the new Christians after Jesus died.

13. (d) St. Dominic (1170-1221) was a famous preacher from Spain. He gathered a band of men who would study, pray, and then preach everywhere they went. This group became the Order of Preachers, also known as the Dominicans. Before he was born, legend says, his mother dreamed her unborn child was a dog who would set the world on fire with a burning torch it carried in its mouth.

14. (c) Tradition tells us that, when the early Church was persecuted and St. Peter was sentenced to die on a cross, he asked to be crucified upside-down. Peter said he was not worthy to die like his Lord.

15. (a) After St. Martin of Tours (316-397) gave half his army cloak to a beggar on a freezing cold night, he dreamed that he had given it to the Lord. He hurried to be baptized, then became a hermit, and later was made a bishop. He was St. Patrick's uncle.

1. St. Clare of Assisi is the patron saint of television because she
(a) invented it (b) had a miraculous vision
(c) was blind (d) was the favorite saint of a pope who liked television

2. The saint in whose memory the Church blesses throats on February 3 is
(a) St. Christopher (b) St. Blase (c) St. Imelda
(d) St. Dominic Savio

3. The saintly woman who cared for the poor and dying people of India is
(a) Blessed Mother Teresa of Calcutta
(b) St. Joan of Arc (c) St. Elizabeth Ann Seton
(d) Mother Josephine

4. The founder of the Benedictine Order was
(a) St. Peter (b) St. Francis Xavier (c) St. Andrew
(d) St. Benedict

5. The name of Mary's cousin who was the mother of John the Baptist is
(a) St. Hildegard (b) St. Jennifer (c) St. Elizabeth
(d) St. Ashley

6. The three angels named in the Bible are Gabriel, Raphael, and
(a) Barbara (b) Michael (c) Dennis (d) David

7. The apostle who was a tax collector is
(a) St. Philip (b) St. Simon (c) St. Matthew
(d) St. John

8. Tradition tells us the name of Mary's mother is
(a) St. Anne (b) St. Joachim (c) St. Martha
(d) St. Louis

9. The strange hermit-saint who lived on top of a stone pillar for more than 30 years is
(a) St. Simeon Stylites (b) St. Bede the Venerable
(c) St. James the Greater (d) St. Rose of Lima

10. The first American-born saint is
(a) St. John of the Cross (b) St. Ursula
(c) St. Elizabeth Ann Seton
(d) St. Margaret of Scotland

11. The apostle whose name was changed from Simon is
(a) St. Paul (b) St. Peter (c) St. Jude Thaddeus
(d) St. Jerome

12. The famous Dominican brother from Peru who deliberately sought the lowest tasks but who also cured the sick is
(a) St. Ignatius of Antioch (b) St. Ambrose
(c) St. Martin de Porres (d) St. John Vianney

13. The Bible says that in the desert John the Baptist ate
(a) meat and potatoes (b) thistles (c) yogurt
(d) locusts and wild honey

14. Legend tells us that the saint who discovered the true cross of Jesus is
(a) St. Nicholas of Myra (b) St. Helena
(c) St. Catherine (d) St. Charles Lwanga

15. The first Christian martyr, a person who was killed for the faith, is
(a) St. Stephen (b) St. Maximilian Kolbe
(c) St. Thomas More (d) St. Polycarp

43

flaum Publishing Group, Dayton, Ohio 45439 (800-543-4383) www.pflaum.com Permission is granted by the publisher to reproduce this page for noncommercial use only.

Saints Almost-Expert Quiz

Answers

1. (b) It was reported in the process of St. Clare's canonization that she was in her sickbed in 1252, when she saw and heard what was happening at the Christmas Mass she longed to attend—just as if she was watching it on television. St. Clare was a good friend of St. Francis of Assisi.

2. (b) Blase was a bishop and physician who was arrested and martyred for his faith. While in prison, he cured a boy who had a fishbone stuck in his throat. This led to the blessing of throats on his feast day.

3. (a) Mother Teresa (1910-1997) was inspired to devote her life to helping the poorest of the poor. She founded a religious order, the Missionaries of Charity, which continues her work. In 2003, she was beatified, the first step to being declared a saint.

4. (d) St. Benedict greatly influenced Church history when he founded monasteries where his followers lived lives of holiness in work and prayer according to his Rule. His twin sister was St. Scholastica who also founded a religious community.

5. (c) Mary hurried to be with her cousin until John the Baptist was born. See Luke 1:39-40, 56.

6. (b) All three are archangels. Gabriel is the angel of the Annunciation, telling Mary that she would give birth to Jesus. See Luke 1:26-38. Raphael, the angel of healing, helps Tobias in the Book of Tobit. See Tobit 5:4-6. Michael, called the defender of the Church, defeats evil in the Book of Revelation. See Revelation 12:7-9.

7. (c) When Jesus called Matthew to follow him, Matthew immediately left the tax booth. He also invited Jesus to dinner. You can read the story in Matthew 9:9-13.

8. (a) Though they are not named in the Bible, tradition tells us that Mary's parents were named Joachim and Anne. They would have been Jesus' grandparents. St. Anne is the patron saint of Canada.

9. (a) Determined to withdraw farther and farther from the world, St. Simeon Stylites gradually increased the height of his pillar. The word *stylites* comes from the Greek word for pillar, stylos. St. Simeon died on top of his pillar, but he inspired others to follow his example. They are known as Stylites.

10. (c) St. Elizabeth Ann Seton (1774-1821) was a wife, mother, and the founder of a religious order. She was very important in the development of the Catholic school system in the United States.

11. (b) When Andrew brought his brother Simon to meet Jesus, Jesus looked at him and said "You are Simon, son of John. You are to be called Peter." (John 1:42) *Peter* means "rock."

12. (c) St. Martin de Porres' powers of healing were so great that crowds came to his doorstep. His great love for humans and animals led people to call him "Martin of Charity."

13. (d) You can read about this in Matthew 3: 4. Some translations of the Bible say "grasshoppers" instead of "locusts." While eating either grasshoppers or locusts does not sound good to us, it was not unusual for people to eat locusts at the time of John the Baptist.

14. (b) St. Helena (250-330) built a church on the spot where the cross was found and also sent pieces to Rome and Constantinople. She was the mother of the emperor Constantine who, in 313, made it legal for Christians to worship.

15. (a) You can read the story of the stoning of Stephen in Acts 7:54-60. Notice that the people who stoned Stephen to death put their coats at Saul's feet. This is the same person who later became St. Paul!

Saints Quiz

1. "On this rock I will build my church" were Jesus' words to
(a) St. Patrick (b) St Thomas (c) St. Peter
(d) St. Jude Thaddeus

2. The place in France where St. Bernadette Soubirous had visions of Our Lady in 1858 is
(a) Lourdes (b) Medjugorje (c) Rome (d) Paris

3. The energetic disciple whose name was changed from Saul and who had a conversion experience on the road to Damascus is
(a) St. Stephen (b) St. Robert (c) St. Germaine
(d) St. Paul

4. The Philadelphia heiress who used her wealth to help the poor and founded an order of Sisters to care for Native Americans and African Americans is
(a) St. Frances Xavier Cabrini
(b) St. Katharine Drexel
(c) Blessed Kateri Tekakwitha
(d) St. Maria Goretti

5. The scholarly saint who led a wild life but later became a bishop and Doctor of the Church is
(a) St. Bartholomew (b) St. Theodosius
(c) St. Augustine (d) St. Angela Merici

6. The French saint in whose honor many parishes have formed societies to serve the poor is
(a) St. Vincent de Paul (b) St. Thomas a Becket
(c) St. Gregory the Great (d) St. Leo the Great

7. The rosary is usually associated with
(a) St. Benedict and the Benedictines
(b) St. Dominic and the Dominicans
(c) St. Francis and the Franciscans
(d) St. Ignatius and the Jesuits

8. The twentieth-century Italian priest who had the stigmata, the marks of Jesus' wounds, on his body for 50 years was
(a) St. Vladimir (b) St. Padre Pio
(c) St. Benedict the Moor (d) St. Kevin

9. The lawyer-saint who was ordered beheaded by King Henry VIII is
(a) St. Thomas More (b) St. Joseph Cupertino
(c) St. Benedict Joseph Labre
(d) St. Maximilian Kolbe

10. The early Church official who was martyred by being roasted on a grill is
(a) St. Paul (b) St. Michael (c) St. Lawrence
(d) St. Albertus Magnus

11. The recently canonized Italian saint who died rather than abort her baby is
(a) St. Gianna Beretta Molla (b) St. Joan of Arc
(c) St. Elizabeth of Hungary (d) St. Agnes

12. Crossed keys are a symbol of
(a) Gregorian chant (b) St. Peter (c) King David
(d) "Keep Out"

13. The saint from Uganda who gave his life in 1886 rather than give in to the immoral demands of the king is
(a) St. Anthony of Padua (b) St. Philip Neri
(c) St. Charles Lwanga (d) St. Charles Borromeo

14. The saint who sacrificed his own life for another prisoner in a Nazi concentration camp during World War II is
(a) St. Thomas Aquinas (b) St. Maximilian Kolbe
(c) St. John of the Cross (d) St. Ignatius of Antioch

15. The sixteenth-century Spanish nobleman who founded the Jesuits and is the patron of retreats is
(a) St. Ignatius Loyola (b) St. Stephen of Hungary
(c) St. Valentine (d) St. Mark

Pflaum Publishing Group, Dayton, Ohio 45439 (800-543-4383) www.pflaum.com Permission is granted by the publisher to reproduce this page for noncommercial use only.

Saints Scholar Quiz
Answers

1. (c) Jesus asked the disciples, "But who do you say I am?" When Peter answered, "You are the Messiah, the Son of the living God," Jesus knew God had revealed this to Peter. Jesus promised to build the church on Peter, whose name means "rock." See Matthew 16:13-18.

2. (a) Thousands visit the shrine at Lourdes every year, hoping to be cured of their illnesses by bathing in the spring that Bernadette discovered.

3. (d) Saul was riding to Damascus to arrest Christians there when he saw a bright light and heard a voice say, "Saul, Saul, why do you persecute me?" You can read about his conversion in Acts 9:1-30.

4. (b) St. Katharine Drexel (1858-1955) used millions of dollars of her family's fortune to establish schools for Native Americans and African Americans. To run these schools, she founded an order called the Sisters of the Blessed Sacrament.

5. (c) St. Augustine of Hippo (354-430) was blessed to have a mother like St. Monica. She prayed that her son would become a Christian, and her prayers were more than answered. Augustine became a Christian, a priest, and a bishop. His writings are considered so important that he was named a Doctor of the Church.

6. (a) St. Vincent de Paul (1581-1660) founded the Congregation of the Missions, an order dedicated to helping the poor, sick, and abandoned. Pope Leo XIII made him patron of charitable societies, including the Society of Saint Vincent de Paul, which still exists in parishes today.

7. (b) The practice of praying the first part of the Hail Mary, called the *Ave*, and repeating it one hundred fifty times began even before the time of St. Dominic. But he and his preachers are known for teaching people to connect the prayers of the rosary with meditating on the events of Jesus' life.

8. (b) St. Padre Pio (1887-1968) was considered a very holy man. He spent long hours hearing confessions and praying for the sick.

9. (a) St. Thomas More (1478-1535) was a brilliant lawyer, a friend of the king, and the Lord Chancellor of England. His conscience would not allow him to approve of King Henry VIII's divorce and his plan to name himself head of the Church in England.

10. (c) St. Lawrence was distributor of alms and keeper of the treasures for the early Church in Rome. When he was ordered to turn over the money and possessions of the Church to the Roman authorities, Lawrence brought with him the poor, sick, and disabled of Rome. These are the true treasures of the Church, he said.

11. (a) Gianna Beretta Molla (1922-1962) was both a mother and a doctor. When she was diagnosed with a large ovarian cyst during pregnancy, her doctor advised her to abort the baby to save her own life. Putting the life of the baby before her own, she refused and died a week after the baby was born.

12. (b) Because Jesus told him, "I will give you the keys of the kingdom of heaven..." (Matthew 16:19), St. Peter is often shown with a key or with crossed keys. Crossed keys are also the symbol of those who succeeded Peter as pope.

13. (c) St. Charles Lwanga and other young men of the court were asked by the king if they were determined to remain Christian. Even though they knew it would anger their pagan king, they said, "Yes!" They were all killed for their faith.

14. (b) St. Maximilian Kolbe (1894-1941), a Franciscan priest, sheltered Polish Jews after the Nazis invaded Poland. He was arrested and sent to Auschwitz, where he received especially brutal treatment because of his faith and ministry to other prisoners.

15. (a) St. Ignatius Loyola (1491-1556) was a soldier whose life was changed when a cannon ball shattered his leg. While recuperating, he read a book about the lives of the saints and was inspired to try to become one himself.

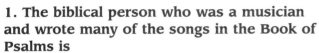

1. The biblical person who was a musician and wrote many of the songs in the Book of Psalms is
(a) Adam (b) Noah (c) Cain (d) King David

2. The Sunday on which the Passion of Our Lord is read is called
(a) Palm Sunday (b) Gaudete Sunday (c) Easter Sunday (d) Pentecost

3. The room at church where vestments and other things used at Mass are kept and where the priest gets ready for Mass is called the
(a) sacramentary (b) sacristy (c) sacrilege (d) vestibule

4. The month we dedicate to the rosary is
(a) January (b) March (c) August (d) October

5. In the Creed we say that the Church is one, holy, catholic and
(a) divine (b) human (c) apostolic (d) pure

6. A nuptial Mass is a Mass for a
(a) wedding (b) funeral (c) Confirmation (d) ordination

7. After the Gospel is read at Mass, we say
(a) "Lord, have mercy" (b) "Lord, hear our prayer" (c) "Glory to you, Lord" (d) "Praise to you, Lord Jesus Christ"

8. Of the following, this is not one of the first five books of the Old Testament
(a) Genesis (b) Exodus (c) Ephesians (d) Deuteronomy

9. Holy Communion given to someone who is dying is known by this special name
(a) liturgy (b) *viaticum* (c) chrism (d) confirmand

10. At Mass, the proclamation "Christ has died, Christ is risen" ends with
(a) "Christ will come again" (b) "You are the savior of the world" (c) "Lord Jesus, come in glory" (d) "Alleluia"

11. "Do whatever he tells you" are Mary's words to
(a) the teachers in the Temple when Jesus was lost (b) the wise men who brought gifts to Jesus (c) the servants at the wedding feast at Cana (d) the good thief on the cross

12. *Abstaining* means
(a) "doing without" meat or another food or drink (b) limiting the amount of food one eats (c) staying up all night to pray (d) keeping strict silence for 24 hours

13. The Church sets aside one day a year to remember all those who have died, and it's called
(a) Halloween (b) All Souls Day (c) New Year's Eve (d) the winter solstice

14. The book approved by the Church that contains the Scripture readings to be read at Mass is called the
(a) lectionary (b) Acts of the Apostles (c) *Catechism of the Catholic Church* (d) Book of Revelation

15. Of the following, the one that was not a plague inflicted on Pharaoh's Egypt is
(a) frogs (b) water turning to blood (c) locusts (d) good crops

Pflaum Publishing Group, Dayton, Ohio 45439 (800-543-4383) www.pflaum.com Permission is granted by the publisher to reproduce this page for noncommercial use only.

Bonus Round Quiz

Answers

1. (d) Even when King David was a boy, his music soothed King Saul when he didn't feel well. See 1 Samuel 16:14-23.

2. (a) We read the Passion of the Lord on Palm Sunday, or Passion Sunday—the Sunday before Easter. We take turns reading Matthew's, Mark's, and Luke's version of the Passion in a three-year cycle. John's version of the Passion is read every Good Friday.

3. (b) The sacristy is usually a room near the altar or near the main entrance to the church.

4. (d) October is the month of the rosary. The feast of Our Lady of the Rosary is October 7. Mary is also honored in May.

5. (c) These qualities are the four essential characteristics, or marks, of the Church. They mark the Church as the one true Church of Christ, serving as Christ's instrument to work for the salvation of the world.

6. (a) The word *nuptial* is an adjective meaning "of or pertaining to marriage or the marriage ceremony."

7. (d) We say "Thanks be to God" after the first and second readings, but "Praise to you, Lord Jesus Christ" after the Gospel.

8. (c) The first five books of the Old Testament are Genesis, Exodus, Leviticus, Numbers, and Deuteronomy. Jews call these books the *Torah*, which means "to teach," and Catholics call them the *Pentateuch*, a word that means "the five." The Letter to the Ephesians is found in the New Testament.

9. (b) *Viaticum* is the name of the Blessed Sacrament brought to a person in danger of death. It means "food for the journey."

10. (a) This proclamation is called the Memorial Acclamation. "Christ has died" is one of four prayers the priest can choose to proclaim the mystery of our faith.

11. (c) Mary's words to the servants are good words for us to remember, too! You can read the story of the wedding at Cana in John 2:1-11. Jesus' changing water into wine was his first miracle.

12. (a) Abstaining from meat is required on Ash Wednesday and the Fridays of Lent. Fasting is limiting the amount of food eaten. Fasting is required on Ash Wednesday and on Good Friday. Both can be voluntary practices of self-denial for other times.

13. (b) We remember all those who have died with the special Masses that are celebrated on All Souls Day. Each priest may say three Masses on this day.

14. (a) The lectionary is usually a big red book with a three-year cycle of Sunday Mass readings and a two-year cycle of daily Mass readings. The sacramentary is the book that contains the prayers and directives for celebrating Mass.

15. (d) When Pharaoh wouldn't let Moses and the chosen people leave Egypt, God sent ten plagues: water turned to blood, frogs, gnats, flies, livestock disease, boils, thunder and hail, locusts, darkness, and the death of the first-born. The story of the plagues is in Exodus, chapters 7-12.